S0-ADC-177

Second Chance Living

Out of the Darkness, Into the Light

Edited by

Linda Ellis Eastman

 **Professional Woman Publishing**
Prospect, Kentucky

Second Chance Living: Out of the Dark and Into the Light
Copyright © 2014 Professional Woman Publishing, LLC
All rights reserved.

Published by:
Professional Woman Publishing
Post Office Box 333
Prospect, KY 40059
(502) 228-0906
www.pwnbooks.com

Please contact the publisher for quantity discounts.

ISBN 13: 978-0-9905418-0-6

Library of Congress Cataloging-In-Publication Data

Cover photo credit: SPOTMATICK/Dreamstime

Printed in the United States of America

TABLE OF CONTENTS

TABLE OF CONTENTS
—CONTINUED—

ABOUT THE AUTHOR

LINDA ELLIS EASTMAN

Linda Ellis Eastman is President and CEO of The Professional Woman Network (PWN), an International Training and Consulting Organization on Women's Issues. She has designed seminars which have been presented in China, the former Soviet Union, South Africa, the Phillipines, and attended by individuals in the United States from such firms as McDonalds, USA Today, Siemens-Westinghouse, the Pentagon, the Department of Defense, and the United States Department of Education.

An expert on women's issues, Ms. Eastman has certified and trained over four thousand women to start consulting/seminar businesses originating from such countries as Pakistan, the Ukraine, Antigua, Canada, Mexico, Zimbabwe, Nigeria, Bermuda, Jamaica, Costa Rica, England, South Africa, Malaysia, and Kenya. Founded in 1982 by Linda Ellis Eastman, The Professional Woman Network is committed to educating women on a global basis regarding, self-esteem, confidence building, stress management, and emotional, mental, spiritual and physical wellness.

Ms. Eastman has been featured in USA Today and listed in Who's Who of American Women, as well as Who's Who of International Leaders. In addition to women's issues, Ms. Eastman speaks internationally regarding the importance of human respect as it relates to race, color, culture, age, and gender. Annually, she facilitates an international conference where speakers and participants from many nations discuss issues that are unique to women on a global basis.

Linda Ellis Eastman is also founder of The Professional Woman Speakers Bureau and The Professional Woman Coaching Institute. Ms. Eastman has dedicated her businesses to increasing the self-esteem and personal dignity of women and youth around the world.

Contact:
The Professional Woman Network
P.O. Box 333
Prospect, KY 40059
(502) 566-9900
lindaeastman@prodigy.net
www.pwnbooks.com
www.protrain.net

Introduction

Linda Ellis Eastman

For unto every life, some rain must fall. However, many women have had more than their share of pain, challenges, and conflicts. If you, the reader, wish encouragement, support, and guidance on your roller coaster called life, this book is written for you.

The authors of "Second Chance Living: Out of the Darkness, Into the Light" have shared personal stories of victory after overcoming pain, abuse, and oftentimes personal trauma. Read each chapter and embrace the lessons learned as the author takes you on a journey from victim to victory!

Second Chance Living

Out of the Darkness,
Into the Light

ABOUT THE AUTHOR

NAOMI D. JONES

Naomi D. Jones MS, RN, CRNI is a Registered Nurse, Certified Life Coach and Inspirational Speaker. In 2005, Naomi started her own company, Consults Unlimited Inc. because she wanted to share her genuine, compassionate concern for future generations. This desire led Naomi to develop coaching programs in Leadership Development and Career Management for nurses. Surprisingly, nursing was not her first choice for a career. She started out as a Home Health Aide when nursing 'captured her soul' and she has been in the healthcare field now for over 38 years. Coaching is Naomi's passion and her nursing career became a natural venue for her to coach hundreds of people over the years. She believes that we should strive to be transformational leaders from within using our mind, body, soul and spirit. As leaders, we can enjoy building our legacy and be effective in changing the lives of others.

Coaching Philosophy

Everyone has the God given right to "prosper and be in health even as the soul prospers." As we develop our mind, body soul, and spirit we can see our choices clearly. Helping people overcome obstacles and find success by transforming themselves is a foundational principle of her coaching business.

Nursing Career

Naomi's practice areas include: Med-Surg, Substance Abuse, Cardiac Step Down, Prison Health, Managed Care, School Health, Hospice and Homecare. She has over 20 years' experience in management and hold a Master's Degree in Health Administration. Naomi served as a Lieutenant in the Army Nurse Corp Reserves.

Other Endeavors

She is a member of the Infusion Nurses Society, National Nurses in Business Association, National Association of Professional Women, Sigma Theta Tau International Honor Society of Nursing, Delta Gamma Sigma Honor Society, Toastmasters International and Lambda Kappa Mu Sorority Inc. Naomi is happily married for 28 years, mother of 4 and grandmother of 4.

Contact:
Naomi D. Jones
1324 Forest Avenue Suite 183
Staten Island, New York 10302
(718) 954-1392
Email: NaomiJones@LifeCoachRN.com
Website: www.LifeCoachRN.com

ONE

When We Know Better, We Can Do Better.

Naomi D. Jones

'I had to settle in my mind to be free, and then allow my soul and spirit to help lead the way for me to get out of the darkness into the light.'
—N. Jones

Dark times exist in many areas of our personal lives. It is not easy to endure some of those times but there is a way to introduce the light of a positive mind, soul and spirit into any dark situation. As women, especially African American women, we need to come out of the darkness into the light. Our cultural history has been influenced by the darkness of slavery since it prevailed in this country. Recognizing how to challenge the perceptions of the past will help all women be better in our own lives and to each other.

Why are we often so disparaging of each other as black women? We live with the pathology of the past. Pathology meaning, any deviation from what is normal. Our past is anything but normal. As a result, when I walk into a room, where only a few black women are; a wall seems to arise as we 'size up' each other, and we simultaneously seek approval from other cultures of women in the room. It is almost as if a kind of distrust exists between us. We need to look at why this phenomenon exists, and come out of the darkness of our past and create a new future full of light and support for each other.

Out of the darkness into the light has to be viewed in its entire context of mind, body, soul and spirit. Darkness has an effect on our entire being. Dark moments in our lives can be very painful and because of that we shy away from thinking about it and prefer to push it into our subconscious. For example, when there is physical, mental or sexual abuse, survivors naturally want to repress the memories in an attempt to stabilize their lives and feel normal. When the survivors do not deal with the impact the victimization had on their lives, other destructive behaviors are manifested. The initial step in minimizing the negative impact for a survivor, is recognizing that they were not at fault and the evil imposed on them was not deserved. In order to be successful in transitioning to light, we acknowledge the darkness but focus on the positive. We can do this because we are created with access to power, love and a sound mind to fulfill a purpose. (2 Timothy 1:7). Even after suffering great disappointments in life, you live and breathe because there is a reason for you to be where you are right now, at this time and in this place. What is your reason for being? How will you turn the negativity around?

Darkness always tries to take over the light both in a physical and spiritual context. I have learned in my life's journey, a little light dispels the darkest of dark. How is light introduced when darkness tries to overtake us? It's a battle and sometimes a war, but we have been given all that we need to allow the light in. What have we been given? Most of all, we have been given freedom of will within our mind, body, soul and spirit. In one of the most influential books ever written, the Holy Bible, states: *"And God said, "Let there be light," and there was light. And God saw that the light was good. And God separated the light from the darkness"* (Gen 1:3, 4) Therefore separation from the darkness is available. You don't have to stay in that dark place mentally or in your soul and spirit. There is always a way to escape. Three ways we can introduce light into those dark moments in life are:

1. Believe that God is.

2. Understand that light is good so look for the good in any situation.

3. Guard your mind and heart from the hurt and pain of the past by focusing on the future and your legacy.

"You intended to harm me, but God intended it for good to accomplish what is now being done, the saving of many lives." —(Gen 50:20)

This a foundational quote for my life. Elders in my community have paraphrased this quote, many times, for as long as I can remember. This quote would help my ancestors get through a lot of hard times and help them find peace in an otherwise harsh environment. Though I have not had to endure the horrors of slavery, when adversity or darkness comes into my life, I find peace in my soul where the truth of this verse resides. There will always be people who will make your life difficult but the power of the promise in these words will introduce light every time even in the darkest situations. Light and darkness co-exist but light will over power darkness every time.

The darkness that pervades our culture as black women is slavery. Slavery in America was not our fault but was based on the greed of others. We still suffer from many of its negative effects, even today, and we manifest it in many ways especially in the way we sometimes treat each other. When I think about slavery, I think about a nation of people who had to figure out how to survive, hold on to their humanity and some semblance of dignity while maintaining a vision of a more positive future. Black women had hope, with every child they bore, that a future for them would include freedom to live the life that God really meant for them to live.

In 2013, the movie "*12 Years a Slave*" won an academy award for best picture. It depicted a story of a free, educated, black man who lived in the north, who was kidnapped and enslaved in the south for twelve years until he got his freedom back. He never gave up in his mind though he had to endure the harshness of the life he was living as a slave. The power of this movie showed the strength and creativity in the minds of the men and women who were enslaved. Many women were creative as they attempted to empower themselves within a system that was designed to take away their femininity and power. In trying to obtain power, some women had to depend on their own individual resources because collaborating together was not allowed.

I think about the many black women who were not allowed the dignity of marriage, used as sexual objects and procreators of future labor. They were made to care for the families of their 'owners' but were not able to give that same care to their own families. They were made to feel inferior to white women. More so, slavery created divisions within our race by skin color (dark-skinned vs. light-skinned) and types of work they did (field worker vs house worker). Historically, society promoted that dark skin was not beautiful. As many women were raped and unwillingly had children from these attacks, lighter skinned children were born. As a result, some women even hoped that their children's lives might be better because lighter skin allowed more opportunities for slaves to gain some status within the system of slavery. Simultaneously, they were bearing darker skinned children within their own family networks which sometimes caused conflict within the immediate family unit. The negative effects of powerlessness and separation by skin tone still impacts the interpersonal relationships among black women today. This is one way the pathology causes us, as women, to be wary of each other. Always 'sizing up' each other to see where we stand as approved or equal within our own culture. We are created to be balanced within our mind, body, soul and spirit and need to judge each other on our merits without these old perceptions.

1 Image used with permission from artist, Ronnie Williams.

Crabs in a barrel represent the mentality of people who are oppressed. This is when people will step over each other or pull someone else back in order to get ahead. Women, in general, were oppressed and that was manifested as negative behavior toward each other. White women were also victims of slavery by being made to **think** they actually were superior to black women while they themselves were often treated as second class citizens by white men. We must also understand the phenomena of oppression. Often the oppressed, when given an opportunity, becomes the oppressor. No one wants to feel the powerlessness of being oppressed so they seek power by oppressing others. White women, who were oppressed, sought power over black women and black women, also seeking power, were oppressive toward each other. This still happens today and is definitely related to years of slavery affecting our mindset as women.

When oppression exists, several mal-adaptive, survival mechanisms occur. One is that the oppressed become invisible. They become invisible to others and themselves. I have spoken to many black women over the years who just want to "fly under the radar." They believe that if they just go about life being invisible or 'good' they will not suffer the retaliatory aspects of racism. Another maladaptive behavior is being silent. Women's voices were silenced within the institution of slavery and it remains a challenge today. I heard an author speak about of a book she had written. She spoke about her grandparents' journey trying to leave the slave culture of the south. She recounted an instance where children were awakened from sleep, hustled into a car in their nightclothes and covered with blankets. They were told not to move or utter a word and if they were stopped they needed to pretend to be sleep. Though they were afraid of being caught and either returned to be enslaved or killed, they still took that risk. Hearing this story gave me an 'aha' moment. For over 200 years, we were taught as a people, from birth that we needed to be quiet, unassuming and silent for our SAFETY! We were taught not to speak up or answer back. It could and did cost many their lives. This continues to be true for the generations of blacks' post-civil war because our safety is still in jeopardy with still existent racism, though it's more subtle.

As women, our voices are continually being silenced personally and professionally. We can turn this around. What we MUST do is silence the culture of oppressive behavior especially among black women toward each other by promoting the good in each other.

Black women are being incarcerated at an alarming rate and taken away from their families. *Voices silenced.*

Incarceration results in the loss of the right to vote. *Voices silenced.*

The glass ceiling for women in business still exists. *Voices silenced.*

Women still make less money than their male counterparts. *Voices silenced.*

Black women still earn less than their white counterparts. *Voices silenced.*

We need to develop the next generation of African American female leaders, coaches and mentors. Give them a voice to stand up for what's right. Encourage them to be visible. Teach the need to have moral courage and to stand up even when their personal gain may be affected. That's the positive legacy we have been left and have the opportunity to leave to others.

How do we introduce the light into our lives and the lives of others? Through personal transformation. Transformation occurs when you willingly change your mindset. *"Do not be conformed to this world, but be transformed by the renewal of your mind, that by testing you may discern what is the will of God, what is good and acceptable, and perfect.*" (Romans 12: 2). That's where you start. We spend a lot of time looking at our jobs, our careers, the way we dress and act and spend very little time reflecting on our lives or our journey. We need to take time to reflect on our past, sort out the details and focus on the good. When we renew our minds to what is good we have light in our lives and we bring that light wherever we go.

You are most powerful when you are authentic. Authenticity will bring in the light. People don't want to look back on our history because of the darkness and the pain. The woman who doesn't know her history is doomed to repeat it. As a culture, connecting the past to the present is crucial for growth. My history is rich because of women who dared to take risks to steal their children away from slavery to points unknown. Women who dared to stand up and demand the ability to choose their destiny and the right to vote. Women who wanted freedom to live as God designed them to live.

What does the present hold for us as African American women? It's a gift that our ancestors have given us and it holds the power of making a difference in our lives and the lives of others. Without understanding your past, the impact you have right now and in the future will not be as powerful as it should be because you will consistently recreate the hindrances from your past. Embrace the past with all of its ugliness and beauty while looking for the good, the power and light within it.

In order to bring in the light and dispel the darkness, don't let the foolishness of others stop you from serving. Let your anger motivate you. Let your fear motivate you. Let your despair, your failures and your successes motivate you. Let all things motivate you as our ancestors did. Decide to choose the path to victory. Let your love, better yet, God's love motivate you. It will inspire you to live your legacy.

Our stories and our history bring value and insight into our legacy that we received *and* will also leave behind. Without telling the stories that have influenced those behaviors, we just have pathology that we keep on repeating to our detriment. If we take the lessons, the strength and successes from our history after acknowledging the negativity, our legacy will be awesome and powerful and bring many into the light.

"You intended to harm me, but God intended it for good to accomplish what is now being done, the saving of many lives." I remember an incident when I experienced moral and ethical pain. A grown woman was standing before me with tears welling in her eyes because she was been made to feel incompetent by a supervisor because of the color of her skin. I had worked at this place for a long time and saw regular patterns of subtle racism being practiced. Knowing the feeling of invisibility and of having the very breath of life sucked out of you, I connected to her pain. That supervisor was attempting to steal her voice. The pain in her eyes propelled me to find my moral courage. This courage enabled me to overcome my own fears and challenge this practice of insidious racism. Moral courage does not come without fear but comes with the need to take risks. Taking that risk actually made a difference in that company and many others found their voice. Risks were taken in many ways by those women who left us their legacy. Women of many cultures took risks to help slaves escape, taught them to read and provided support to those who needed it. One thing I have learned in my journey is that the color of someone's skin won't tell you whether they will treat you with respect and as an equal. My advice, judge the heart and actions of a person not the color of their skin. What motivates you?

We are born with the innate desire to live freely. Every human being wants to be seen, heard, loved unconditionally, cherished and protected no matter what race or gender we are. Guarding your heart and mind will help you live in the light. Embrace your life where you are. Be thankful for your opportunities to grow whether those lessons were painful or not. Use those lessons and apply the knowledge. You will grow in wisdom, which is, knowledge applied.

As women we come out of the darkness into the light when we use our knowledge to make better decisions and choices. We can choose to have moral courage and take risks to bring in the light and help others no matter what color their skin is and we need to be especially good to each other as black women. When we challenge the darkness and move into the light, we will no longer live the pathology of our past but will live in the victory of creating a positive legacy. You are here for a reason. We only have a season and there is no work in the grave. Live into the future through the lives you touch today. We no longer need approval from other women or have a need to size each other up. We can freely serve each other as we remember what was given to us.

Our journey is a series of second chances. As long as you wake up and remember who you are, you have another chance to live out LOUD.

My eyes were opened and I had a second chance at living when realizing I come from Kings and Queens whose strength, power and leadership is what allowed my people to persevere through the horrors of slavery.

My eyes were opened and I had a second chance at living realizing the strength of a woman is in her ability to feel compassion.

My eyes were opened and I had a second chance at living realizing that a woman's body is built for the miracle of continuing the life cycle of humanity.

My eyes were opened and I had a second chance at living when I knew and understood the unconditional love of my God towards me and His amazing care of everything that happens in my life.

Looking back on my life I see the hand of God protecting me and directing me toward the fullness of my purpose in service to others. Embrace the positive aspects of the legacy you have been left. Enlighten your mind, soul and spirit with lessons from our past so you can answer the question: What's He keeping you for?

ABOUT THE AUTHOR

DR. CYNTHIA PARKER WHITE

Dr. Cynthia Parker White is a native of St. Petersburg, Florida. She is a 1970 graduate of Gibbs High School. She went on to earn a Bachelor's Degree (1973); Master of Arts in School Counseling (1979) and Certification in Educational Leadership (1998) all earned at the University of South Florida, Tampa, Florida. She earned an Educational Specialist degree in School Counseling (1995) from University of Southern Mississippi, Hattiesburg; Education Specialist in 2004 and Doctor of Education in 2005 both in Educational Leadership from Argosy University, Sarasota, Florida.

She is currently employed as a Professional School Counselor (34 years) at her alma mater. She has served as an adjunct professor in the Counselor Education program at Argosy University /Tampa, Florida specializing in Social and Cultural Competencies for Educators (Diversity) as well as other courses needed for program completion.

She is a member of Zeta Phi Beta Sorority, Florida school Counselors Association and Pinellas Professional School Counselors Association and serves on the Board of Governance for Community Action Stops Abuse (CASA). Dr. White is also a member of the Professional Woman Network, an internationally recognized organization where she trained and earned certification in Diversity and Women's Issues.

She is the author of Healing for My Hurt: A Journey to Wholeness/Finding My Father, Finding My Self and Big Boys DO Cry: The Struggle of Growing up Black and Male. In addition: How to Break the Glass Ceiling without a Hammer: Career Strategies for Women (Co-author, Understanding & Embracing Diversity); Leaders in Pearls: How to Be a Change Architect (Co-author, Overcoming Racism & Creating Inclusivity in the Workplace) and Boys to Men: The Guide for African American Boys (Co-author, Dealing with the Pain of the Absent Parent) all PWN books.

As a woman of faith, her battle cry is Jeremiah 29:11 which states, "For I know the plans I have for you, declares the Lord; plans to prosper you and not to harm you; plans to give you hope and a future" (NIV).

Dr. White is the President/CEO of Dr. Cynthia Parker White & Associates, LLC, a consulting firm conducting seminars and workshops on women and family issues.

Contact:
Dr. Cynthia Parker White & Associates, LLC
P. O. Box 13226
St. Petersburg, FL 33730
P.727.656.8271

TWO

My Sister's Keeper

Dr. Cynthia White

Every morning I arise at 4:00 a.m., carry out my morning ritual of getting dressed for work, reading my morning devotional and at around 4:30 a.m. Eastern Standard Time, sending out from my laptop, daily inspirations to slightly over 50 women whom I count as my sisters. This is my practice Monday through Friday of each week, holidays and summers included when school is out and I get a brief reprieve from the grind of work. I established this pattern nearly four years ago as my way to connect to other women. I always feel that I need words of encouragement and affirmation to help me get by sometimes moment by moment, particularly when my chin might be dragging the ground and my faith tank is running a little low. My group is comprised of women of different ethnic and cultural backgrounds, various ages and from different walks of life. As far I know, most if not all of us are of the Christian persuasion. Some I have face to face contact with on an ongoing basis while with others it is more intermittent. Some of them respond back to inspirations that especially touch them or strikes a chord by sending a return email back to me confirming that the words have hit their mark. Some I never hear from but they have not openly said stop sending the daily words of comfort and affirmation meant to help in getting them through whatever life challenges that may be confronting them.

For me, this very act was a step of faith as it had been difficult for me to cultivate but a few limited friendships with women, particularly my African American sisters. The reason were many but predominantly, I felt that they would not understand my journey or the challenges and obstacles that had shaped my life. I bore shame for many of the struggles including having been in an abusive marriage. I was too immersed in blaming myself for being in the situation that sharing with other women was not an option I considered. For a very long time, I isolated myself, not feeling particularly comfortable with attempting intimate friendships with other women. I struggled with lack of self-worth, low self-esteem and lack of self- -confidence despite the success I had achieved through hard work.

I came to the realization that the feelings and emotions I had internalized were shared by many other women. It is unfortunate indeed that we as women have unwittingly cultivated a history of not trusting each other, not looking out for each other, or looking to each other for comfort, for strength and for encouragement.

In the book of Genesis from the Old Testament, comes a familiar story of two brothers Cain and Abel, the sons of Adam and Eve. Cain took the life of his brother as a result of jealousy and envy. When God asked him, "where is your brother Abel, Cain replied, I don't know, am I my brother's keeper?" We know the rest of the story and his fate for his evil deed.

The answer to Cain's question is a resounding yes; we are indeed our brothers' and our sisters' keepers. If we need further evidence, we can look to the scriptures again from the book of Mark, 12th chapter and verses 30-31 which state:" And thou shalt love the Lord thy God with all thy heart, and with all thy soul, and with all thy mind, and with all thine strength; this is the first commandment. And the second is like, namely this, Thou shalt love thy neighbor as thyself. There is none other commandment greater than this" (KJV). The same care and concern that Jesus had for us that commended Him to die on a cross is the same love that we should have for each other. It is the kind of love that says, I want for you what I want for myself. It is an unselfish love that rejoices in the triumphs of others and likewise feels the pain and suffering when another is going through a valley experience.

When we look at the words of Cain in Biblical times and fast forward to the future, we can see our own unwillingness to extend ourselves on behalf of others and assuming responsibility for the wellbeing of our fellow human beings; regardless of their conditions or station in life. The challenge is to overcome and bury that me and my mentality; the selfishness that lurks within and says, I have mine, you get yours the best way that you know. We are not called upon to help those willing to continually take and who are unwilling to help themselves. These are individuals always looking for a handout rather than a hand up so that they in kind may help another.

You might not be a blood relation of mine but I love as if you are and as a result of that love, I have it within me to always strive to render aid and comfort, always looking out for others to the best of my ability.

As I have grown older, I have learned to value my friendships with women more highly. I tended to isolate myself in my younger years and built a wall around myself that prevented others from getting too close. All I could visualize were my perceived flaws that the rest of the world and certainly other women could see. My life experiences made me feel unworthy in so many ways. My isolation from other women was a misperception that I was unworthy of their friendships and their love. I reached out to help other women but would not allow others to reciprocate. At some point in my life I began to yearn for that affinity with other women and realized that in order to have sister friends, I had to let down my guard and allow other women to see the real me who was suffering but striving at the same time to heal and to become whole.

When taking the time to share my own story, my struggles and my victories, women began to share their stories in return. I came to realize that so many other women were hiding behind their own hurt; some the same as my own; some vastly different but hurt no less. This speaks generally and specifically to women and what we endure. We all have our battles, our own demons but they are made worse when we single out each other for additional hurt. We are hurting and we allow traits like jealousy and envy of each other to take root and have dominion in our lives. Rather than championing and cheering each other on, we employ the crab mentality of me first at all cost.

What remains is a distrust and distaste for each other; a tearing down instead of building up when what we really want and need is the reassurance that we are not alone; that we share common ground with other women and that if we can be open, honest and trusting of one another, we can all seek and find the path that would give us peace from the pain we have each endured on our life's journey.

As women, I think we should possess a special calling to reach out and feel the cares of each other. As a woman of God, I believe strongly that I am my sisters' keeper.

This scripture speaks generally and specifically to women and what we endure. We all have our battles, even our own personal demons but all of our struggles are made worse when we single out each other for additional hurt. We do it to each other because we are jealous and we are envious of each other. We are fearful of reaching out and determining our own destiny but resent those who face their fears and achieve success.

As I have lived my life, grown in maturity and wisdom, I have been allowed to see the need for bonding with and building the sisterhood. From my vantage point, sisterhood transcends race and color and even cultural difference. I perceive all women to be my sister no matter how young or how old.

Therefore, my passion has become reaching out to as many women as I can and encouraging them to reach out as well to the women they encounter in their own circles. In a world becoming more and more devoid of compassion on many levels, we as women need each other for support, for reassurance, to stand in the gap for us and to pray for us when we cannot pray for ourselves. We need other women who understand our valley experiences, when we are in the worst moments of despair as well as those who encourage and applaud us when we land on the mountaintop and taste the sweet victory of accomplishment and success. As women, indeed as sisters of the heart, having each other's backs should be a given with no fear of being lied upon, turned on, deceived or betrayed.

Building relationships of love and trust with other sisters need not be a difficult task; the building blocks for connection are already present. When we are hurt, tossed to and fro by the challenges and pitfalls of life; we know exactly what will comfort us. If we do for our sisters what we would like done for us, the walls that divide us would begin to crumble.

Our stance should be that every woman is our sister. They do not have to biologically be our sisters, but they certainly can be our sisters in our hearts. It should not matter to any of us that some might be African American, while others might be White or Hispanic or any other color of the rainbow; it matters only that we are bound by the things in life like our love and deep respect for each other, our mutual commitment to family and a prevailing love for our Devine Savior who is the giver of all life.

It is our sisters who give us joy and make our hearts laugh and our souls happy. They are the ones who should cause us to shed tears when they are in the midst of suffering and pain for truly we are our sisters' keeper. Thus, when they hurt, I hurt and when they rejoice, I rejoice with them.

I have lived three score and two years and have come to realize that there are far more things that connect me to my sisters than things that divide us. I have learned that a mother's heartache transcends the boundaries of race and color when she is alienated from a child she has brought into the world; nurtured only to have that child stray far from the path of their upbringing and perhaps even disavow you as parent. Skin color does not matter when one loses a beloved parent or spouse or suffers the heartbreak of a shattered marriage or relationship. Hurt and brokenness know no boundaries thus they don't single out by size or shape or color or creed. Thus I have learned that every woman is potentially my sister and I am hers.

The society in which we live would have my sisters and I believe that we are as different as the night is from the day and that nothing in our lives speak of the commonalities that we actually share. It is our undertaking to change core values within our society that would have us believe differently. No longer should we perceive each other as enemies but as allies. As women, we are the primary bearers of culture, knowledge and change in society. We have within us and among us as women, as sisters, the potential to abandon what is customary and institute a new order whereby we resolve to unite as one to preserve ourselves, our families, our communities and the larger society. The sisterhood of women has the power to change the world order particularly if we focus upon our shared characteristics and traits rather than the few things that we can count as differences.

I have cultivated many friendships with women through social media. Some live near and others live in countries across the globe. As I am perusing statuses on Facebook, I often read the comments of women who are hurting and reaching out for comfort and confirmation that they matter. Sometimes the post will be hours old and no one would have commented. When I see such posts and read them, I always think of that woman in the manner I would like to be thought of. I need to be stroked from time to time; to be built up when I have been torn down in my personal or professional life. I want to not be invisible and for someone to "see" me and reassure me that despite the current storms, a better forecast is coming and that I need not endure alone.

Before the opportunity presented itself to write this chapter, I had participated in dialogue with some of "my" sisters about what sisterhood meant to them, whether it was biological or sisters gained along the way. The topic of building and perfecting the sisterhood was heavy on my heart. I was conducting formal research but I also wanted to hear firsthand from other women their personal experiences and thoughts on the subject. These are the thoughts they shared with minimal editing to protect the integrity of their words:

Brenda F

We need to be able to unite/come together as sisters. It could be going to church, out to dinner, lunch, prayer groups, etc. and continue to show true love toward one another. We don't have to wait for a funeral, a wedding or a reunion, it should be just because. Support one another in feelings, if someone is having a hard time & you know it don't talk about them behind their back in a negative manner & then turn around & smile in their face. Pray for better days ahead, & if someone gets a promotion at work, in church or community, show them some love, don't be a "Hater". The list goes on & on, perhaps someone else can shed some light, to get some of our sisters out of the dark & into "The Marvelous Light".

Barbara T

I love my sister girlfriends. We have seen each other through the highs and lows of life. We walk together for exercise, we have breakfast most Saturdays. There is nothing else like my sister relationships. We understand what we go through as women, as mothers; as wives to men who betray us or who fail to be what we need them to be. We celebrate all that is good and that is special to each other. Without them life survival is very difficult. We can be more open with each other and honest about whatever. The things we talk about can be down-right scandalous at times! Then there is that completeness of spirit. I guess like Gail and Oprah, we are similar. There are three of us. I sincerely believe all women need this type of support.

I found Barbara's assessment to very much on track. What she has with her three besties, I pray that we all could have and we can if we break down the barriers that separate us, vow to love and trust and never betray, not even for a man. Our ultimate goal should be partnering with each other to perfect our sisterhood. Barbara's relationship with her "sisters" captures the essence of what sisterhood is all about. You three have created inseparable bonds with each other that are mutually satisfying and beneficial.

Kathleen W

Cynthia....Hello, You know that I wholeheartedly agree with the comments from Barbara! We as sisters need to support one another in whatever...not needing a man to validate who we are! We also need to learn to appreciate ourselves! Many women (Sisters) find it hard to appreciate themselves because society puts pressure on us to be completely selfless; any attempt at self- nurturing and self-love is condemned! We must develop the ability to embrace ourselves as well as one another! Now you know y'all got me started now! We need to hear from more of our sisters!

We most definitely need to hear from more sisters. As I said, healing the sisterhood is a passion that should consume each of us. Many of us have great relations with each other and other women but some of us don't trust each other, don't like each other and purposely hurt and use each other.

Women need to hear from sisters like these so they know what we are missing, and what we can have with each other. I have a biological sister who is 15 years younger than I am. We are as different as night and day; she is the crazy one who will kick butt and go to jail for her big sister if she had too. I love her to pieces but in reality, she is not necessarily the one I can tell my fears and dreams to. I have a "Sistah" friend who is my soul mate; the one who understands the introvert that I am and knows just when I need a hug. We both lead very busy lives and sometimes don't get together, but we miss each other and realize that we need sister time together. I would do pretty much anything for her and know that she would do the same. I look to her to pull me back on track when I am too far out there. I have a tendency to withdraw and retreat into myself. My "Sister" sees that, understands it and knows the perfect moment to intervene. She is my confidant and I am hers. She holds a delicate position so she knows that I one hundred percent have her back and would never betray her trust. For her and all my sisters, we have an unspoken yet sacred bond and oath of silence between each other. I have other Sister girlfriends whose personalities are totally different; we fulfil needs in each other's lives that are also different. We live hundreds of miles apart and often go long periods with only cursory interaction but the bonds are no less strong and when we come together, it is as if we never parted. I love the fact that we can disagree but never be disagreeable towards one another. I recall how when I lost my mother, on the day of the services, they all showed up. I looked up and there were just there. I am not certain who made the call, but they were there. And likewise when others in the sisterhood lost a parent, the rest of us showed up. The looks on their faces at seeing us there most likely matched the look on mine in my time of need.

As I grow older, my Sisters assume an even larger role in my life. I need them for my emotional well-being and I believe that they need me in like fashion. Some of us have been a part of each other's lives approaching fifty years. We have known each other through elementary, junior high, high school and college. Some of us have married, had children and divorced. Some have remained single and childless but the ties remain. We have nursed each other through countless heartbreaks, medical crises, financial misfortunes, two house fires and countless other mini tragedies.

What I am most proud of is that we are all women of faith. It is our faith and trust in the Living God that has sustained us individually and collectively. Regardless of how we worship and what name we attach to our religious experiences, we can all attest to the fact that we would not have made this far without the Lord on our side.

And so me and my sisters, we laugh together, we have cried together and in our younger days, we have partied hard together. Many of us have been long separated by miles but not even distance has been able to wear down or wear out our relationships with each other. There is a popular gospel song by Hezekiah Walker entitled *I need you to Survive* that speaks poignantly to the relationships that need to exist among women. In part, the lyrics say:

I need you
You need me
We're all a part of God's body
Stand with me
Agree with me
We're all a part of God's body
It is his will that every need be supplied
You are important to me
I need you to survive

I pray for you
You pray for me
I love you

I need you to survive
I won't harm you
With words from my mouth
I love you
I need you to survive

True sisters love each other; they pray for each other and never speak words of hurt or harm for in all aspects of life we need each other to thrive and survive.

Notes:

_____

_____

_____

_____

_____

_____

_____

_____

_____

_____

_____

_____

_____

_____

_____

_____

_____

_____

_____

ABOUT THE AUTHOR

Ms. Jacqueline P. Wilson

Jacqueline Wilson is the President and Chief Executive Officer of The Wilson Life Skills Institute. She conducts empowering workshops and seminars that consist of topics such as; Save our Youth Today for Tomorrow, Social Etiquette, Leadership: Your Path to the Future, Entrepreneurship: A Way of Life, Teen Image Awareness, Financial Literacy and Communication Skills for Everyday Living, the Responsible Fatherhood Initiative Program and Life skills Training for workplace and personal development.

Ms. Wilson has been certified by the Professional Women Network as a Professional Coach, Youth Trainer, Women's Diversity Coach, Entrepreneur Trainer and Teen Image Consultant. She has also been certified by the National Partnership for Community Leadership as a Master Trainer for the Fatherhood Initiative Program and by the Nurturing Fatherhood Program as a Nurturing Father and Marriage and Relationship Trainer. She is also certified by the American University for Neuro Linguistic Programming as a Master Life Coach specializing in the field of transition coaching.

Jacqueline's knowledge of business, leadership, teamwork and communication is supported by working with and within various organizations. She has 26 years experience in Information Technology; 15 years in the Financial Sector, 11 years in the Health Care Sector of which the last 10 years were in Project Management, still within Information Technology and 6 years as a volunteer in the Bronx Fatherhood Program as a Life Skills Facilitator.

Ms Wilson also has a program for Women In Transition that assists young and mature women who are making changes in their life as relating to Divorce, Domestic Violence, Leaving the Prison System and Total Life Change.

Among her various accomplishments, Jacqueline has co-authored a book, holds certifications in Telecommunications from DeVry Technical Institute in New Brunswick NJ and Business Project Management from NYU in NYC, NY. Jacqueline is currently a New Jersey State Licensed Bail Bond Agent with her own agency, Lady J Bail Bonds, LLC. Her main primary focus is juvenile prisoner re-entry.

Books:
    Co-Authored: Life Is An Attitude…..The Power of Positive Thinking
    Co-Authored: Second chance Living

Certifications from Professional Woman Network
    Certified Professional Coach
    Certified Youth Trainer and Coach
    Certified Entrepreneur Trainer and Coach
    Certified Teen Image Consultant
    Certified Women's Diversity Trainer
    Certified Women's Empowerment Coach
    Certification from American University of Neuro Linguistic Programming
    Certified Master Life Coach

Certification from National Partnership for Community Leadership
    Certified Master Trainer – Responsible Fatherhood Initiative Program
    Certification from Nurturing Fathers and Marriage and Parenting Program
    Nurturing Fathers
    Marriage and Parenting
    Certification from Women Aware - Middlesex County, NJ
    Domestic Violence Training

Professional Organizations and Affiliations
    Toastmasters International
    NAACP – Bergen County, NJ Chapter
    National Organization of Black Law Enforcement Executives   **(NOBLE)** – Northern New Jersey Chapter
    Affirmative Action Advisory Board of Teaneck, NJ

Contact:
Email: twlsi@live.com
Office: 888.201.6203 x4
Mobile: 917.763.4939
Fax: 201.708.6540
Lady J Bail Bonds, LLC
Email: ladyjbailbonds@live.com
Office: 888.707.9886
Fax: 201.708.6540

THREE

Moving Forward... Seven Years Later

Jacqueline Wilson

When we are born, we all have something that we must overcome. It's not always drugs or sex or alcohol. It could be pride, arrogance, stealing, or anything that is not pleasing to God. We must all escape that thing that holds us back from moving forward. The thing that keeps up locked up in our own personal prison. We do get a second chance at life every second of every day of our life that day we are on this planet. It's available to you. Do you want it?

Today is May 26, 2014. The last three of seven years has been such a wonderful time for me. This has been a time of learning, a time of getting to know myself, a second chance at living for God.

When you think about second chance living what comes to mind for you?

To me it meant that I had a chance to get things right in my life. I had to look at every choice presented to me and every decision that I had to make and to determine which way to go. But, I did not do it alone. The Holy Spirit was with me each step of the way, leading and guiding me.

Since everything is about God in my life, I have become sensitive to His voice. What lessons will I learn along the way? Will I get things right this time? Well, that is the goal.

My prayer is for you to consider looking at where you are now. Determining if that is where you want to be and if it is not where do you want to go?

Consider your last seven years.

How Did I Qualify To Get A Second Chance?

According to the scriptures it says that it is the Lord's mercies that we are not consumed, because his compassions fail not. They are new every morning: Great is thy faithfulness. **Lamentations 3: v22-23.**

Just with that scripture alone tells me that I get another opportunity to get things right in my life. Now what I do with that opportunity?

As a Christian, it is imperative that we rely on God to succeed in life. It's crucial. I did not fully believe anything I just mentioned to you. After all, I had the life I wanted. But I clearly remember God saying to me after I had gotten married a second time and I quote "If you would have waited six more months you would not have married him." I had always pondered what He said to my heart but put it in the back of my mind. After all, I was happy and had everything that I wanted. But slowly that relationship was slipping away.

A few years later in July on a bright and sunny day; "I don't want you to follow him, I want him to follow you". I thought to myself, where am I going and where is he going? What a strange saying. I had no idea what God was talking about. That day I found out that my spouse was planning for us to move to Florida. His job was going to be relocating and he wanted to go with the company. Do you see the dilemma? Needless to say for 18 months there was constant friction because, I clearly heard from the God not to go.

Question:

If God gave you a directive that would cause you to seemingly lose everything you had in the natural, would you obey His voice? Yes or No and explain your reason.

_____

_____

_____

_____

_____

There was one thing that I know and that is when God speaks to me audibly, He definitely wants my attention!! When the fullness of time came I had a decision to make. Go with God or Go with Man. It was an extremely tough and emotionally painful decision but I decided to go with God. I whole-heartedly believed that He would fix my marriage, especially since he hates divorce. And when that didn't happen I was very angry at God. I could not see what He saw. For four years I would serve Him in the church but with an angry heart. How could you let my life fall apart? I trusted you. You said that You would not leave me or forsake me. You said that Your mercies were new every morning. I prayed and obeyed Your command. My life was in a tail spin. But I clearly heard the voice of God and no one could tell me otherwise. So why was my life going this way? I have lost everything, everything except my mom, job, home and car. My mom kept speaking the word to me and my job kept me busy. What a combination. The ending of my second marriage led me on the journey of my life. After all the pain, shame, guilt, anguish, broken heartedness and being homeless temporarily, I learned a few things along that way I want to share with you. It's all about God, moving me forward, seven years later.

Knowing The Voice Of God

According to James 4:8 the scripture says; Come close to the one true God, and He will draw close to you. Wash your hands; you have dirtied them in sin. Cleanse your heart because your mind is spilt down the middle, your love for God on one side and selfish pursuits on the other.

When you start to increase your reading of the Word of God this is one form of drawing closer to Him. It allows Him to speak to you through the scriptures. It is His love letter, life skills training and problem solving technique manual for us. So that we are to live victoriously on the earth to accomplish His will for our lives.

According to **Psalm 46:10** He says be still and know that I am God.

You accomplish this by being quiet from all distractions. God is a gentleman. He is not going to speak over your phone calls, kids, TV, conversations with others, etc. After all we wouldn't like it if we were speaking to someone and they had distractions going on while we were attempting to speak to them.

When you set up your daily time to pray and meditate God will speak to you at that time as well. He wants to be close to you. He wants to fellowship and have a relationship with you.

Who Am I?

For some people this is a loaded question. We often listen to others tell us who we are, or we define who we are. For example, we say that we are a waitress or secretary or landscaper or Vice President or CEO or hairdresser or manager or a bum, etc., etc. This is how someone else has classified us. In actuality that's not who we are. Those titles are the role we play in a business or on a job. It's our job function. It's NOT WHO WE ARE. We are Christians. We are a CHILD of the most High God, made in His image and likeness. That's who we are and you do not forget it. Never let anyone tell you who they think you are. It has already been decided from the foundation of the earth and solidified when you accepted Jesus as Lord and Savior of your life. Even Jesus wanted to know who men said that He was. Consider the following scriptures: **Mark 8:27-29**; Now Jesus and His disciples went out to the towns of Caesarea Philippi; and on the road He asked His disciples, saying to them, "Who do men say that I am?" So they answered, "John the Baptist; but some *say*, Elijah; and others, one of the prophets." He said to them, "But who do you say that I am?" Peter answered and said to Him, "You are the Christ." Get the point??? If you know who you are then no one can call or label you something other than who you say you are.

Talents, Skills, Strength and Weakness What Am I to Do?

I had to look at my life and all the things that I have done well and enjoyed doing. And what were the transferable skills and talents that I possessed to create a new life for myself. If you remember from my first co-authored book, Life Is An Attitude, The Power of Positive Living, I decided on a career in Information Technology. In my 26 year tenure I had several positions that required various skills and talents. Those skills would lead me to different career path or career advancement in Information Technology. I made an assessment of all the skills talents that I had acquired during my career and this is the list I came up with.

Leadership, communication skills, team building, project management, organizational skills, time management (I'm still working on this one), budgeting, coaching, mentoring, public speaking, humility, understanding the four personalities, vendor management.

See what I mean? I did not learn any of this all at once, put over a period of time. Also it's not about just learning, it's about putting things you learn in to action.

It's now time to list your strength, weakness, talents and skills. Your strengths will help you to excel in life. Your weaknesses will become strengths in the future and training points for you to better yourself now.

List Your Top 5 Strengths:

1. _____

2. _____

3. _____

4. _____

5. _____

List Your Top 5 Developmental Areas (Weakness):

1. _____

2. _____

3. _____

4. _____

5. _____

List 5 Talents and Skills You Have:

1. _____

2. _____

3. _____

4. _____

5. _____

Are You Open To Change?

One of the things that I had to do was to get more into the Word of God and fully understand that He has my best interest at heart. The scripture says in **Jeremiah 29:11**; For I know the plans I have for you," declares the Lord, "plans to prosper you and not to harm you, plans to give you hope and a future." So I'm thinking to myself "ok now what Lord". I have lost everything that I treasured. I'm following You. Now what? When I started reading more and learning from other messengers that He placed in my path things started to change for me. Life, for the first time, was becoming more and clearer to me. All of the hurt, guilt, shame and other negative emotions that I had accepted into my life were now leaving. And each day after that life became more appealing to live. I had a business partner that would always answer the phone "It's a Great Day to Be Alive." I hated when he said that because my life was a mess. I couldn't understand why he was so happy and grateful. Until that day when I started truly understanding God and why He mandated that I not move to Florida. But first I had to want to change and to learn more and to be more and to want more. This is when change happens.

Are you open to change? Yes _____ or No_____

If not, Why?

_____

_____

_____

_____

If yes, what changes are you committed to making today?

_____

_____

_____

Understanding Others

In order to understand others, we must first know and understand ourselves. We must allow ourselves to be transparent so that people will really see us. No one has gone through anything that someone else has not. There is nothing new under the sun, nothing at all. Knowing this, being honest with ourselves and others allows us to understand what someone else has gone through. This allows a door for us to open, enter in and assist someone else. It's called being empathetic.

When my husband and I separated I felt lousy, irritable, sad, mad, etc.

I went to the gym to work out with my trainer. At the end of our session she begins to tell me about how her boyfriend broke up with her and how miserable she was without him. Of course, I did not want to hear that, after all I'm in the same situation. But what God prompted me to do was to tell her what I was going through. I didn't want to do that because I was a private person and I was more ashamed and embarrassed than anything. So I went into the trainer's locker room and told her my situation. We hugged and guess what, she felt better. Not because of an apparent loss that I was going through but because she was not the only one going through that type of situation. I felt better because it was a release for me and I knew that I was not the only one who had been in a broken relationship.

Being able to relate to someone is huge. People need to know that at some level you can relate to what they are going through. You can empathize with them and can encourage them. We are all here to help someone else reach a higher level. We do that by having compassion one for another. Once there is a level of comfort we can start to empower someone else to be the best they can be. This is actually a movement. Each one, reach one, to teach one.

The World Around me

As my life now has changed from being married to single, I had to re-adjust things. I now go out alone, to the movies alone, food shop alone, clean the house alone, I have to drive myself where I want to go, I attend church alone (well I was already doing that), everything is in single mode now. There are no kids, no laughter, nothing. This is no the life I wanted but guess what? I started to enjoy my new found freedom. For the first time in my life I am able to get to know God without distractions. I am able to grow and mature in Him. I am able to see things in the world the way He does. I am able to do the things that God wants me to do. I can speak to and go where he wants me to go to do His will. As I allow Him, He is leading and guiding me in all truth and taking me to another level I had never been to before. Showing me the various world's within this world. Now I'm living!!!

God allowed me to see the various worlds within the earth realm. It was actually scary. People were just busy doing things that did not matter in the greater scheme of God's plans for mankind. If we are not doing God's work, then what are we doing? Surely we are not helping our fellow man.

Since I started to really commune with God and build a relationship He showed me things from His view. At the same time pointing me in the direction He wants me to go into, all for my good and His plan. Remember **Jeremiah 29:11**

Who Is With You?

I have learned that being honest in dealing with people and yourself is the key if you wa;nt to get ahead in life. I learned that everyone on your bus is not there for the same reasons. Some will get off the bus before you, some with you and some after you. But you must know when it's time for you to get off the bus, purchase your own bus and drive it. I learned that everyone is not what they seem. Talk to a person for 5 minutes and you will know where they are coming from. Talk to them longer than that and they will have you following their philosophies.

Always Stay true to you and true to God. Not everyone is going along with you in this life journey. And that's ok. People are in your life for a reason and a season. Don't get upset when they leave. Just let them go, God is in charge. Always remember that everyone has their own journey in this life.

What Have I learned?

My second chance in life came by way of making a decision to release a relationship, take a new job, learn new skills, embrace the leader that I am and helping others along the way.

As I became more comfortable with myself and seeing that God has been there all along for me. He has been giving me chance after chance to make the right decisions, which are His decisions for my life. Doing this has made things more clear for me as I now know what His Will is for my life. I know what I am supposed to be doing in life. He has introduced things into my life subtly as to not shock me or make me run off. God changes our heart slowly if we let Him like a rudder on a ship.

Today, I am involved in the Prison Ministry at my church. Not in my wildest dreams would I have thought of myself speaking to anyone in prison about anything and enjoying it. We are all prisoners of something. We have to find our path to break free and to live the life that God wants for us. I have learned that anyone can change their circumstances at any given time by submitting to the high calling from God.

LAST TIDBITS

1. How do you handle obstacles and challenges?

_____

_____

_____

_____

2. Everyone needs to be centered. What avenues will you take to get centered in your life?

_____

_____

_____

_____

3. What would a second chance at life mean for you?

_____

_____

_____

_____

4. What does being a leader mean to you?

_____

_____

_____

_____

5. What are your aspirations in life? What is your passion?

_____

_____

_____

_____

6. What must you give up (maybe temporarily) to get to your predestinated position in Christ?

_____

_____

_____

_____

Remember, never give up, trust God always, submit yourself to Him and you will have the desires of your heart because He cares for you.

He that comes to God must believe that He is and is a rewarder of those that diligently seek Him. —Hebrews 11:6

Moving Forward...... Seven Years Later

I had no idea seven years ago that I would be where I am today. Not in my wildest dreams. My Father God has taken my pain, sorrows, mistakes and negative thinking and has turned it around for His good. He has placed me on the path to success for His glory. Now my mission is to bring someone else along.

Believe it! Believe it! For it is true, that God does love you. Open your heart, let Him in and watch Him transform your life. No turning back, no turning back!

In Jesus Name Amen!!

Notes:

_____

_____

_____

_____

_____

_____

_____

_____

_____

_____

_____

_____

_____

_____

_____

_____

_____

_____

_____

_____

ABOUT THE AUTHOR

ZENOBIA BAILEY

Although I come from a family of several educators, I find it interesting that I never intended to make education my career of choice. However, I was afforded a challenge and an opportunity to embrace it as a second career. It's one that I've passionately pursued.

The first African American Master's candidate admitted to the University of Iowa's journalism program, I credit the broad shoulders and dedication of my parents and grandparents. They are my giants and I owe everything to them. While I have no doubt that I am indeed one of their second chances, I know full well that it's because of them that I was afforded even my first chance, allowing me to pass the baton to all three of my living second chances. They are Shamar (32), Jared (30), and Julita (26).

After more than 20 years as a home educator, [delete and] teaching in three other colleges/universities, a private school, and substituting in Metropolitan County school systems, I am currently teaching Principles and Strategies of Successful Learning for the University of Maryland University College. I am also a life and wellness coach who happens to reside in one of the most beautiful places in the United States - the Pacific Northwest. I live there with my husband and best friend, Irwin. I affectionately call him *Dad*.

Contact:
Zenobia Bailey
637 S. 32nd Pl
Renton, WA 98055
(800) 804.3604
zenobiabailey1@aol.com
https://www.lifecoachhub.com/coach/zenobia-bailey-m-a

FOUR

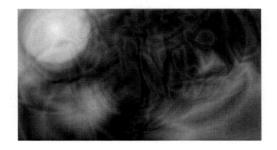

Second Chances

Zenobia Bailey

Second chances come in all shapes, sizes, colors, and presentations. They are availed to everyone. We just have to look or ask and then receive. Sometimes, they're not even second chances. Instead, they are third…fourth…fifth, or far greater.

How many chances have you had? How many have you taken advantage of? If, by chance, you feel they've not come your way or at least not in awhile, I challenge you to stop right where you are, at this very moment, and reflect on your day thus far. What comes to mind? Write it here: _____

Why is it a second chance? _____

_____

What impact will this second chance have on you today and/or in the future? _____

_____

Day by Day...

Seasons...years...months...weeks...days...hours...minutes...seconds...even mini seconds encircle our lives. With each tick of the clock a phenomenon that is totally untamable occurs. Time literally moves and cannot be reclaimed. While many refer to their age in years, others speak in terms of seasons. Staring at 70, I'm considered to be in the late autumn of my life.

Over six decades of innumerable second chances! The most important evolved out of my questioning nature which has existed as long as I can remember. *Why and how do you know* punctuated my young life and continued into my teens and adulthood. Without a doubt, something deep within was missing and I felt that if I could resolve this question that perhaps I'd have the key or at least a place to start.

When I was between 11 and 13, I began to actively search for answers to explain why we were here. By the time I enrolled in graduate studies, I was sure that I'd pieced the puzzle together with the help of Carl Rogers. To my grave disappointment, I thought I was moving forward only to learn that I'd fallen victim to even more confusion which caused my queries to grow. My search, although it seemed pointless, continued for another year or so.

Two roads diverged in a wood, and I —
I took the one less traveled by,
And that has made all the difference.
—Robert Frost

I will never forget the wee hours of November 23, 1975. My friends Ariam and Lear traveled two and a half hours to share something they called "vitally important." They had no clue where I was on my journey. In fact, Ariam knew my questioning and debating nature as we'd attended undergraduate school together and she didn't really want to approach me. Still, she told me later, she felt that she must.

How glad I am that she and her new husband Lear did indeed get in their car and purposely sought me out. It was this act that opened the door, allowing Christ to come into my heart and take up residence. It gave me THE second chance. Ariam and Lear showed me from the Bible that I was separated from God because of sin and that because God did not and could not co-exist with sin I needed a Savior. The Savior was Christ who had died to rescue me (and everyone else). "However," they patiently explained, "Christ will not force himself on anyone. You must ask him to forgive you for your sin, tell him you want him to be your Savior, asking him to live in your heart". Revelation 3:20, *Bible*. Guess what? I did.

Have you? _____

_____

No thunder clapped. I didn't walk on clouds. However, I felt the weight of the world lift off my shoulders and knew, without a doubt, that although I couldn't explain it, this was where it would begin.... where the answers to my life-long questions would begin to come together. I deem this transformation my largest and most important gift that I will ever receive. Why? It's because it opened the doors that allowed scales to fall from my eyes to see people and things in ways different than I'd myopically seen them; to accept others and even circumstances; to forgive and love large; and to fully embrace others as I want to be embraced. These newly acquired attributes have allowed me to experience and in turn grant many second chances.

Loss and Grief...

We cannot escape the reality and effects of divorce, separation, betrayal, or death. At times, some of us seem to get more than our share. I've stood with others in each of these instances and I've walked through more death situations than one might ever think she'd see in a life time. News of the *Big C*; a call in the middle of the night that a neighbor's twin girls have been picked up and charged with multiple felonies; opening a letter to find that a spouse no longer wants to be married. The list of loss and grief can be inexhaustible.

Nine years ago, my Dad kneeled at his sofa with me on his left and my Mom on his right to ask the Lord to show us how to trust. Although he was terminally ill and wracked with pain, Dad taught me yet one more lesson in a litany of lessons regarding what it meant to take every opportunity and make the best of it. You see, in less than an hour, he was rushed to the hospital. Two hours later, he began to drift, eyes disoriented. I called the nurse who, in turn, loudly and forcefully called his name. I watched my Dad re-orient. Then, from seemingly nowhere, one and a half hours later, my Dad left us. I often find myself reflecting on his action and words right before we left for the hospital. They inspired me then and they inspire me now. I hope they always will.

I've just returned from a visit with my Mom. We live on opposite ends of the country. Along the way, Kasia, an excellent therapeutic massage therapist, offers me much needed recovery from my flights. For the last six years, after each visit with Mom, I've asked the Lord to allow me to see her one more time. He's granted me many second chances. I'm grateful for each knowing that sooner or later, if I survive her, I will have to face another incident of loss and grief.

It doesn't matter how these companions visit us. We are thrown off our feet, drenched with confusion, as we are reeled back and forth grappling with denial, anger, bargaining, depression and acceptance which are considered the five stages of grief. Sometimes, one stage over-rides all of the other stages. At other times, not all stages raise their heads. And, there are times when additional stages are referenced. The point is that no matter how many stages we engage, they are very necessary to help us place one foot in front of the other, getting us to another second… minute…day…week…month…year…to yet, another chance.

It Is the Darkest Before Dawn...

"We must tell people that no pit is so deep that He is not deeper still".
—Betsie ten Boom, *Any Where He Leads Me.*

Lana describes how Child Protective Services came into her home in the middle of the night. *"They grabbed my 18 month old baby out of my arms without a coat or blanket and took her out into the cold February morning. They walked past me and my husband to my older daughter's room who was 12 at the time. She was awakened and whisked away as well."*

Lana and her husband had recently moved to the area from an upper mid-west town. They knew no one. However, Ethan remembered the banker who'd recently helped him. This is how my husband and I came to know and befriend Lana and Ethan. We also knew the banker who shared the plight of this young African family who were very unfamiliar with this American practice of extracting children from their parents. By the same token, we didn't know much more than them.

However, that all changed as we walked with them through the accusations, inquiries and court dates. We advocated for them and their family, even gathered signed petitions and media attention. By now I'm sure you must be asking, what happened? To be honest, I'm still asking that question as are Lana and Ethan.

Ethan's 14 year old daughter Elle is Lana's step-daughter. Yet, Lana treated Elle as her birth daughter and had no indication that things weren't well between them. **B E T R A Y A L** rang very loud and very clear! Elle told her high school home room teacher and principal that her parents regularly performed African cutting rituals on her body.

She described the process in detail including the "fact" that Lana would hold her down while Ethan used an extremely hot knife.

It is impossible for me to describe the agony this situation brought to the hearts of Lana and Ethan. I'd just met them but I felt the intensity of their pain, not only the loss of their children but the need to come to grips with the serious breach brought on by the false accusation made by their daughter. It literally knocked them off their feet. All I could do in those beginning days as we worked together to develop a strategy to move them forward was sit with and minister to Lana in every way I knew in order to meet each second, one by one, in preparation of taking hold of her second chance.

Lana and Ethan faced seven months' separation from their daughters, watching them being moved from one unacceptable foster home to another while allowed only 45 minute visits each week. Lana's heart literally broke, reducing her to tears, each and every time she witnessed her infant daughter's dirty clothes and unkempt hair. Worse than that was the foster Mom's attitude about it all.

The two younger children were reunited with their parents and are enjoying their second chance. Lana says, "*It's still hard today. I still have huge questions about this system and the fact that it employs professionals who, with all their training, were and remain unable to decipher truth from fiction in situations like this. The bottom line is that this accusation remains on my record and interferes with my ability to move around freely. People from other countries worship the US until they arrive and actually live here, experiencing various injustices. We leave our countries looking for a second chance and although we receive it in some ways; we're stripped of it, in others.*"

I found myself fully entwined in a situation that exposed a system that charged this couple without investigation. I saw prejudices and predispositions towards a culture very different than ours up close, naked and vulnerable. I witnessed a couple who had run barefoot in the middle of the night in order to escape rebel attacks in their birth country, now encircled by fabrication. I especially watched Lana. This same woman, who crossed the borders of two other nations in order to get their children to safety, was now being accused of harming her children. How in the world does one walk, even run from the center of one state or nation to another with their children? What are your thoughts?

_____

_____

_____

I believe it takes a determined will along with hope and faith. Yet, each of these had been displaced with brokenness, hopelessness, and despair. Using this experience, the Lord whittled me into someone who would be willing to take a chance and listen beyond words, beyond the situation, to hear the heart of one in need. With time, forgiveness sprouted in the midst of this serious crisis. In the end, Lana was rescued from some very deep waters and I gained a treasured friend who I'd not have otherwise met.

"The word of the Lord came to Jeremiah a second time...I will tell you (currently) hidden and unknown things." —*Bible*, Jeremiah 33:1-3

Light and Life: Battling Darkness and Death...

In June, 1971, President Nixon declared the war on drugs. Since that time, countless individuals and families have been struck by the ravages that typically accompany their illicit use. My family is no different. A cousin sampled the wares as an experiment. It was very costly to him and all whom he loved. This is his story:

Chemical Dependency ran a lengthy course in my life. With that said, consequences seemed unbearable. The destruction brought a measure of unlawful acts and a prison sentence. Serving the allocated time in prison also presented a new found freedom. I could see a needle eye opening of relief. Oddly, I found freedom from within; a second chance for a different and better life in the making. During my incarceration, I met several people who perceived something good in my persona and worked with me.

When I think about a second chance, forgiveness is key. I have been given many chances and opportunities. I recall being rushed to the emergency room with a temperature of 105. I had been ingesting an enormous amount of narcotics, hoping to feel better or at least numb the pain.

The ER doctor announced the test results. "Mr. Franklin, good and bad news. You have a severe case of pneumonia. You're not going to die today. However, you have H.I.V. In 1984, this was a death sentence.

Once discharged, my addiction took off to its highest heights. I wanted to go to sleep permanently. I held the SECRET for five years. The drugs eased my pain momentarily. I began to shoplift, steal and cash checks trying to quench the thirst of my habit. Within a short period I was arrested and sent to prison. Crazy as it seems, I felt a relief from all the chaos and drama. This incident brought me to my knees. I was offered a new found freedom, leading to the opening for a second chance.

Who has the right to with-hold a second go at it from anyone? All people are fallible. Life is a road trip, full of lessons. Oftentimes, one may get the wrong map. Following the map of deceit, will throw anyone off course. One of the greatest gifts one can offer to another individual is forgiveness.

Joy Comes in the Morning: Forgiveness Continues...

"Without forgiveness, there would be no real second chance. It would have been fool's gold, non-profitable. I realized that I loved my Dad when I saw his addiction to drugs. And, forgiveness came with the experience of letting him parent me at the age of 17." —Terrie W.

Terrie, one of my mentees, granted me permission to share the quote above and the following:

I've come to see that I was a troubled, immature, and lost teenager with blinders. I now see my contributions and responsibility in what developed into a bad relationship. I know that I didn't make things easy for my Dad, at all. Neither of my parents had ever shown unconditional love to me as a teen. So, I looked for acceptance in the world. In return, I found more hurt. Once the world had disappointed me enough, I believe God used the timing to usher in my second chance.

My Dad was clean for almost a year and through a number of seemingly unfortunate circumstances, I found myself being offered his care. While he was excited, I didn't have another option and had little to no excitement. However, as the days and weeks passed, I saw a different man. His openness allowed me to trust and forgive him. We built a relationship of love and respect. Before his passing, I was proud to have this man as my father.

Second Chances: Intergenerational Legacies

We are all conduits along our various journeys. Addressing the subject of second chances, I must acknowledge the lives of two phenomenal women. Lealia, born in the early 1900s, was the oldest of eight children. Although a math genius and quite the student, across the board, she was needed in the cotton fields and Ladies' kitchens in order to help her parents care for the basic needs of the family. Still, this determined woman saw a second chance for her son who imparted his vision of the passages, mostly financial, that would be required. Against all odds and with insurmountable sacrifice, Lealia mounted the necessary funds for the initial gateway that clicked again and again, leading to the crowning of a PhD in nuclear physics and chemistry for her son.

Ophelia, born in the late 1800s, birthed nine children and adopted one. She enjoyed a few more privileges than Lealia, including the ability to complete her education and become a school teacher. In the process, two of her children followed in her footsteps, becoming educators. One became a principal, the other a teacher. Lealia and Ophelia are my wise and loving grandmothers. Both were conduits for change and second chances for countless, including me.

As we part, I leave you with this: *"Left to ourselves, we're mud pies baking in the elements of preference and prejudice"*. Beth Moore, *James: Mercy Triumphs.* My friends, it's always about choices, no matter what the *it* is. A very wise woman whose husband had just kissed her on the cheek, prior to going outdoors to enjoy the fresh air, never returned. Without any illness; any warning, he collapsed on their terrace. One week later, she stood at his home-going and shared, *"It doesn't matter what happens to me. Rather, it matters how I respond."*

Bam! Those words pierced my entire being. This is why, without hesitation, I can pen them 25 years later. They were another doorway that would be foundational to unconceived second chances. I remember how I tried and even tested God in the early days. What I didn't realize at the time was that God, unlike us, keeps His word. I've found that He always met me exactly where I was, step by step. Over and over again, I continue to find Him faithful.

Notes:

_____

_____

_____

_____

_____

_____

_____

_____

_____

_____

_____

_____

_____

_____

_____

_____

_____

_____

_____

_____

ABOUT THE AUTHOR

KAREN DONALD

"Everyday is a second chance at life!" This is the personal testimony and mantra that is so often and eloquently spoken by Karen L. Donald. As a result, Karen stands boldly today as a beacon of triumph and victory. However, the road that this powerful woman has traveled to get to this point would make the average person cringe as if viewing a horror movie.

She endured rape, molestation, and mental oppression from community leaders and members of clergy. This, in turn, caused her to internalize the pain associated with the theft of her innocence. Karen's personal battles led to drug and alcohol abuse, depression, abandonment, and the carousel ride of one toxic and destructive relationship after another.

Today, Karen is an Minster, Speaker, Author and Business leader. With meetings throughout the United States and Africa and Central America already under her belt, Karen has set her sights on further delivering the word of hope inside of her to the world. She is expanding into different forms of media via radio, TV, internet, and producing countless edifying products to heal the total man.

As an established entrepreneur, Karen founded Donald and Associates in 2000. As CEO, with over 20 years of Multi media experience, sales training, coaching, marketing and advertising, Karen has formed a team of specialist across the Globe to not only handle the needs of clients in the United States but Internationally.

Karen L. Donald is truly a woman of personal victory. This awesome woman, global business leader, dynamic life-coach, wonderful mother, and restored person is truly taking advantage of her victory and is sharing it with the world!

For more information regarding Karen L. Donald visit her web site at:

Contact:
www.karenldonald.com
Twitter and Facebook: Karen L. Donald

FIVE

Free To Be Me!

Karen Donald

To say we want to free and actually being able to walk in that freedom are two very different scenarios for many people. As a Life Coach and Spiritual Counselor I have found that one of the biggest areas of moving forward into ones second chance is the first step. There are so many internal challenges that will hinder someone if they have not allowed a sort of deliverance from denial of the past to take place; mind, body and soul.

The mind is the central station of what you will do. Thoughts and imaginations can and will take over your success in reaffirming your life. What you think you are. There is a verse in the King James Version of the Bible that says in the first sentence, (Proverbs 3:27), "As a man thinks in his heart, so is he." So little words, such a big definition. No matter how "free" you really believe you are, you must first believe that you are just that. Some of the most successful people in the world will say that they thought and then became or did what they saw. No matter what your past defines, you have to be able to see or think of yourself in a better place in life. You have to know for sure, no matter what anyone else says, that what you have left behind is gone and it is Ok to move forward. Great examples of this are those who suffered from addictions, alcohol, even abuse. There is so much tied to these behaviors, that for a long time people cannot let them go. A drug addict, for example, does more than just use a particular drug. Often times, a person that has heavily exposed themselves to a drug also has other behaviors that follow: theft, lying, guilt, shame, poverty, sexual promiscuity and more. So when a person is in rehab from drugs and/or alcohol, all the other attaching emotions can begin to come to mind. Those alone can cause a person to fail at the process of rehabilitation and starting fresh. The same with alcohol abuse. As a person that has been abused, many times the person has been led to think that the abuse is there fault (guilt). They won't find anyone else that will love them (shame), everybody that knows they have suffered in this area has talked about them, laughed at them and called them crazy (false imagination). Again, these emotions can be very strong and without the right support and exercising the mind of rethink who you are, you will always believe that you are that same person.

As a person who suffered from abusive and addictive behavior in the past, one of the most difficult hurdles to get over was the guilt from my past actions. I often wondered or thought that someone would remember me and not consider me for a job or opportunity because of my past actions. There was no way for me to see the power in the story and the fact that it was now a testimony. Even with speaking engagements, training programs and praise I received for my accomplishments, I always looked at myself in the mirror as that girl who I used to be. That alone cost me time and energy; and also made me create lies and excuses not to move forward. When in actuality, the person(s) or organization I was going to see needed to hear my story and have my professional advice and experience. Not too many coaches are fortunate to have both. When I opened my eyes to that realization, it was up from there. I had to take a real strong look mentally at who I was emotionally, physically and know that it was time for me to walk in the freedom that I'd gained years before. I had to walk guilt free and without shame, no matter what others had to say about it. When your are making you move into your new you, there will always be someone around to remind you that you were not always that person. I guarantee you it will be a close friend, relative that will wait to express as loud and strong as they can, "I remember you when you were, or I remember what we did." I suggest you get your "ready" sentence rehearsed until it slips out of your mouth like a routine. Mines is "Yes I do too. I am so blessed to be here and have my second chance!" Not feeding into there thoughts of you will make them find something else or someone else to move on to. Most people that do not celebrate others are intimidated by your success and wish they could have it to. When strong enough, you can offer some suggestions and give some tips to others. This will actually make you stronger. Every time you share your story, whether big or small, it builds self pride in what you have accomplished for yourself. Until then, smile, give your sentence and pat yourself on the back. You did it and now you are in a new season of life! Self awareness is an important factor to a healthier mind. When you look at yourself in the mirror, make sure that you are speaking positive affirmations and staying true to you. Your biggest fan is yourself. Celebrate your accomplishments and get ready for a new life! Remember, your mind is the filter for what your body and soul feeds upon. In the same, your mind will react to what your body is doing and feeling. As you begin to do exercise your mind, now you will have the feeling of wanting to take charge of your body.

The body is a very important vehicle. It stores the very essence of who we are, all different for different purposes in life that we were individually created for. In my visits to wellness coaches, there is always a focus on the body. If we are to travel, work or function in the household, our body has to be able to function as well as possible. When you are beginning your second chance, you may notice some slight differences in your body that you don't remember from before the trauma, abuse, additions or just life circumstances. Stress, fatigue and depression, just to name a few, are emotions that can have a damaging effect on your body minute to minute that we never see until it's too late. It is up to you to take charge and have your mind made up to take charge of your body and decide what you want to see your next phase look like. If you've gained a few pounds, lost too many pounds, see some changes in your blood pressure or just feel tired all time, take the challenge in your new state of Freedom and make plans to make a change. Contact professionals and see what you can do to change your diet. Join a fitness gym and work with a professional trainer if needed. The changes in body appearance can be very difficult ones to face without support. You may also want to have a partner to help you to achieve your goals just by having someone to listen too. In your time of change and second chances, look at yourself as a temple of hope for not only you, but for someone else. You may also look at your body beyond weight and health in gestures, stature and grace. We are so unaware that different circumstances in our lives are projected through our body movements or language. Have you ever been so tired or have a slight cold that someone you don't even know can watch how you walk or look and be able to mention it or question you about it? Our body language also shows attitudes; some of them not always nice or pretty. When we are angry or having a problem with what someone said or did in our presence, we tend to react. Being free and beginning your second chance, you will want to keep conscious notes on your reactions whether in person, by phone and other forms of communications. A greeting card can trigger old memories. There are people in your lives that may not know how to react to your change and really say something that can disturb you. When you do not understand what a person meant by their words or actions, make sure you ask before you react. Everyone has an uncomfortable moment when words just did not work. Even when starting over from a loss of a loved one or illness. It is not always a comfortable subject, although a close friend or relative would love to have a motivating conversation. A long stay away because of hospitalization, rehabilitation or our moments of trying to bounce back. Remember that the topic as bad as it could be for you most times is worse for the other party. Some will feel guilty because they were not there to help or because they had not tried. Those people will always be the ones that will try to accuse you of becoming angry or reacting in a bad way. What happens most of the time is that they have found a way to hide bad intensions or shame by making you feel that way. Letting them know that you are a better person and that you are making your life better everyday will push you and them past the fears and open the door to a dialogue that will be empowering for all. While working with your body, remember a tip that I give in all my classes. Who you are on the inside will always show on the outside; eventually. So when you find yourself reacting in anger, bad body language, headaches or high blood pressure, go back and look at what triggered it. Learn to identify what bothers you or what you react to and keep track of those feelings.　Allow yourself to continue to heal emotionally from what you have encountered.　Healing can take place alone, at a place of worship, through support groups, counselors/ coaching and more.　If you do not allow yourself the time to work on yourself and be happy about your accomplishments, you can find yourself bouncing back; and that is not an option.　I recently met with a client that, in my minds eyes, has recovered from Alcohol addition. Why do I say "has"? As his counselor and now friend, I always work to share positive affirmation in my interactions.　So when I knew he had a drinking problem, I could see it because of my own past.　I never mentioned to him that I knew.　I just remembered him in my prayers and also gave him a warm greeting, pat on the back and told him that this is going to be a better day than yesterday.　When he decided to tell me what was going on, I waited until the right time to respond in the fact that I knew.　I did it by not saying I could detect it, but I told him that I always thought about him and prayed for the best, because that was also my struggle and I knew what it looked and felt like.　With that response, he became comfortable to share his story with me and told me how long he had been sober.　This was a fact in which I could see the very month he started that goal.　What is so powerful is that he decided that he had to stop drinking because of his adult child who was picking up the same habit.　He did not want that to be his child's demise and wanted his child to look for a better future.　He found hope in helping someone else, which is very important.　After about 6 months, he began to look and feel better,　but during the holiday months and times that families come together, I would leave him a message, send a note or make a call to let him know that he has done a great thing and it is ok to be free.　The days I am around him and his body is having bad reactions to his new found freedom, I remind him, better days are to come, give him a hug and a big positive smile. It is important beyond your understanding that everyone around you is now there to celebrate you, no matter what it looks like. The next area that I would like to end with is the: soul. The soul is the spiritual side of who we are as men and women. It is the strongest of the mind, body and soul trio because it is the core of who we are. The soul controls why we think, the way we act and the things we say. Your personality and your being, is your soul. So the wisdom, thoughts, creativity and your dreams, just to name a few attributes, are part of your soul. During our challenging times, it is the soul that can become the most damaged. Although a person can suffer from a mental illness or even a physical illness, you will find that it has a lot to do with a person not being able to find themselves and ending up in a bad or unfamiliar situation. Unfamiliar to what? The who that is inside of you; your soul. For the healing of the soul, you must allow for a spiritual transformation to your original state of thinking and being. In your worst times, there are always dreams inside of you that you are yearning for, if even in your imagination. That is because the person you were created to be is always there until you pass away. During this time of your life's resurrections, your number one goal will be to have an opportunity to fulfill your destiny, live your dreams and have ultimate happiness. None of which anyone can give you, it begins with you. The who we are on the inside is what we always strive for. That is why you always hear people say, "I just wanted to belong to something". So in a moment of fear and rejection, a person may find themselves in places, with people and doing things that are so out of their character and soul seeking to find a happy place within them selves. I love the idea of food for the soul. There are rich actions that cause us to feel better about life and who we are. I believe that such actions are liberating because it is who we are and meant to be. No matter what faith, religion or background, most can believe that we were created and have a reason for being here. What the reason is can be pretty hard to resolve some days because it was not put in a manual so to speak for us to follow. If you believe that you were created to lead, dominate and be a help to others within our space, I believe you are on the right track. While you are working on your new lease on life, let me share with you some powerful tools that I have found rich food for the soul. Love, a very dramatic and many times harsh four letter word because it carries a lot of weight. However, when you love what is connected to you through your soul, there is a harmony that will take place. Many will say that love is the opposite of fear, not my thoughts. I truly believe that love, hate and unforgiveness are in the same emotional triangle. Because of the hurt that can be connected to love, fear can come into the grouping because your future love may be shadowed of the fear of the past. Unconditional love that is given through the soul and offered through our being has nothing attached but that. So you can love through your daily works, actions, giving and kindness. Sharing the wisdom that is placed inside of you comes from your soul being. It feels good to talk and share with others what you have discovered about yourself, the world and current events. Some information was stored in you from generations. You may hear someone say that you remind of them of an old family member that you never met, because wisdom is a part of our DNA which is made up of our soul, which is also defined as our character. My family always teases each other because we all have something to say. We tease each other all the time, but it is important to get it out, it feeds those three big areas; mind, body and soul! Another source of nourishment for the soul is learning the art of forgiveness. Yes, the big

F. it takes many of us to another place that we really do not want to deal with. It is a two way street, especially in beginning again. Not only do we have to forgive others but we also have to work on forgiving ourselves. In our life's battles, we make many mistakes and there are others who have made mistakes that were not necessarily for us, but caused us the greatest pain. Right now you are thinking and nodding your head. Usually someone closest to us is our attacker or who we attack. I say we, because I only write, speak or lecture on things that I truly can relate to; forgiveness is a subject that has given me a lot of experience on both sides of the fence. Without forgiveness, you can never be truly free because it is so liberating in itself. Each moment you remember without forgiveness, you will live the pain over and over again. True forgiveness takes steps, which at times will mean to confront the matter head on. Now, I do truly understand that it is not always convenient to face the person, place or thing. Some have not forgiven those who are no longer physically with us, but we continue to carry the pain of that act or past. Also with the process of forgiving yourself. Wow, a huge one. You have to not only looked at who you are, but also face your past actions and what pain it might have caused to another person. The worst of that is the fact that you may never see the person again. I can hear you going, yes Dr. Karen, Yes! Ok, for those who are ready to figure this one out, I am going to give you a real easy key. Going back to love, it is the most comforting emotion of the human soul which helps our body and mind. Being able to walk in love will allow your spirit to look and see what happened, resolve the issues within and lean how to not only to forget, but to forgive. If you don't combine the two, one will always show its face. Your space in this universe depends on forgiveness to live in harmony, detaching yourself mentally from the pain. That pain can manifest itself in body, mental and heart felt agony.   Another area is the creative part of your soul. Your desire to paint, make jewelry, even cook. Most chefs are the happiest when someone else enjoys their food. They sit, smile and wait for your reaction. When you are happy eating, they are happy cooking, much like the older men and women in our lives. They love to cook huge meals traditionally for holidays or special occasions and watch everyone enjoy! That is comforting for their soul and ours! Our soul was also developed for giving and helping. For the most part, we are happy when we can volunteer for a cause, mentor someone or just find someone to share with. It is usually a "pay forward" based on our hearts desires to be appreciated. Giving unconditionally, without reason can be the best feeling in the world! When you can give to someone who does not know you specifically or someone who totally needed a touch that day, you feel as if you are on top of the world. Honest charity from your heart, which is an attribute of a healthy soul. Begin to give small acts of kindness and allow others smiles and words of gratitude warm your spirit. Your soul can be healed if you are ready. It was created to love, give, offer peace, smile, laugh and have a rich life.

The very essence of who you are throughout time and even those who will follow you in your blood line lies in your soul.

In conclusion, coming into your second chance living is a wonderful place to be. God has given you the opportunity to live again, the way you want to. I offered information about the three elements of the mind, body and soul, because as cliché as it sounds, it is who we are. By being alive and being here and now, you are able to share your gifts to the world and work towards your life purpose which is ultimately your destiny. You hear and read a lot about understanding your purpose, how to define it and where do you start. I want you to lean on me now and begin to live right where you are. The blessing in your "now" is that you are alive and breathing air that has been given to you as a gift. Use that gift of life and just be you, the person you have been looking for, calling for and hoping would show up. Take interest in who you are and have become. You have the right to call yourself a winner, an achiever, a survivor and a champ! You can embrace that person in the mirror every morning and say "good morning" to the best looking person I know. I am alive, free, walking and standing. I might have lost a lot, but I did not loose me! I might have cried many tears, but my joy has come to me today. People might have said that I would never make it, but here I am, a living testimony of not only making it, but making it in a great way. I am _____ and I have been blessed with a second chance. Today I am free to be me, because that is who I was created to be! Enjoy your new lease on life and remember that everyday you live is a second chance at life!

ABOUT THE AUTHOR

CHARMAINE M. SMITH

Charmaine M. Smith, is President and CEO of EMERGE, PLLC a Personal and Relationship development company committed to equipping and empowering individuals through their own choices to live fuller, more productive lives, particularly in the area of relationships.

Licensed psychotherapist in the states of Kentucky and Texas, Charmaine is passionate about the SELF improvement, SELF renewal and SELF discovery of individuals and conducts personal and relationship development seminars engaging a combination of transparency and straight talk about overcoming relationship 'red flags' in efforts to ignite individuals to break free of self defeating behaviors, habits and relationships. Charmaine's motto is, "*The moment you settle for less than you deserve, you will get even less than you settled for*". The Co-Author to two previously published PWN books, **Learning to Love Yourself: A Handbook for the African American Woman** and **Learning to Love Yourself: Self Esteem for Women**, Ms. Smith is also the producer of an inspirational, spoken word CD for women entitled, "EMERGE". Currently, Ms. Smith is penning her first self published book entitled, **Relationship Café: 30 Mindful Truths to Consider** with anticipated release for Spring 2015.

A Summa Cum Laude graduate from the University of Maryland Eastern Shore, Ms. Smith also earned a Master's degree in Marriage and Family Therapy from the Louisville Presbyterian Theological Seminary and is an approved Marriage Enrichment facilitator by Family Dynamics, PREP and Life Innovations. As a psychotherapist with proven experience working with conflicted couples and at-risk adolescent males and their families, Ms. Smith is highly in demand as she evokes a unique blend of sensitivity, insight and depth with the capacity to engage her clients in solution-focused, strengths-based, results-oriented therapeutic services.

Born and raised in St. Thomas, US Virgin Islands, Ms. Smith is a member of the American Association of Marriage and Family Therapists, the Kentucky Association of Marriage and Family Therapists, Phi Kappa Phi, the National Association of Female Executives (Women on the GO Network) and the Professional Woman Network (PWN).
Contact:
Charmaine M. Smith
President, CEO
EMERGE, LLC
P. O. Box 6697
Louisville, KY 40206
www.Emerge2Day.com
CharmaineSmith@Emerge2Day.com

SIX

An Intimate Meeting with Stevens-Johnson

Charmaine Smith

"There is really never a good time to be ill, but this had to be the worst time... If I had known what was coming, I would have felt the price was too high to pay" —M. Hunter

The metamorphosis of a butterfly has always intrigued me....yet I only fully grasped the marvel of this transformative process in my life when I met Stevens Johnson.

January 2011 was an anticipatory time for me. My staff and I had just completed a plethora of collaborative Holiday community service events and projects – and I was elated to afford them approved holiday leave to enjoy memorable moments with their families. Amidst of all the jovial 'wooing' associated with the commencement of a New Year, everyone proclaiming New Year's resolutions spreading across the gamut from loosing weight to getting married, my entire focus was on my upcoming 40th birthday celebration in Orlando, Florida. Excitement and expectancy fueled my days. *February 7th* could not come soon enough.   My plans were made, double checked and reconfirmed. For me, forty signified a self-loving transitional season. Opening decades of my journal writings, I said to myself *if anyone would have told me growing up* that I would bury my mother at age 18; suffer brutal domestic violence; face community scrutiny; forfeit a full scholarship to law school; be married, then unmarried; change careers; relocate for serenity and safety and finally end up ministering to masses of women, teaching relationship seminars, writing books, impacting the lives of thousands multi-stressed families and couples - and raising a confident, phenomenal and beautiful daughter, I would have stopped the speaker immediately with the burial of my mother and asked for a personal consultation with God for a re-write of this script BUT in reflection I was grateful for the journey because it helped me to understand the transforming power of the Divine. HOWEVER, as I counted down the days to February 7th, embracing my decision to live more fully and abundantly, the thought never entered my mind that my life was about to collide with a major unexpected twist.

It was a Thursday. A winter chill filled the atmosphere. The corridors of the agency echoed busy chatter of dedicated service professionals posturing for another 'ordinary' work day – but – January 13th will forever be etched in my memory as anything BUT ordinary. Sporadic fever spikes and blood shot eyes propelled me to leave the office by early afternoon with a medical appointment scheduled for first thing Friday morning. That eve, I took allotted Tylenol, rubbed myself down with Vicks VapoRub, drank frequent fluids and slept in a sweater and socks in an attempt to fight the germs attacking my body. Friday morning, my eyes were eclipsed red, fever was 106 and there were three circular red marks across my upper chest. The circular red marks were literally burning my skin. Yesterday, my initial thought was I possibly had pink eye. Hence, I was prepared to get the prescription medication and stay home for the specified time noted by my doctor but the red circular marks across my chest throw a wrench in that notion. Needless to say, at the doctor's appointment, the physician confirmed that it was not pink eye. *Okay, then what was it? I have no time to be sick. Let me know so I can get on with living and planning for my 40th birthday.* I was sent home with a prescription for eye drops to alleviate the itching and redness, instructions to continue with Tylenol for the fever and a simple request to stop using the Vicks VapoRub on my skin and the marks will disappear. *I will admit the request to stop using Vicks VapoRub was hard for me to accept as Vicks VapoRub has been a miracle medicine necessity in my family for generations – and never has my skin been irritated or reflected any allergic markings as a result of its use.* Well…straight way, I dashed to Walgreens, filled my prescription and complied with the doctor's orders *including stopping the use of Vicks VapoRub.* I also remained in bed for the duration of the day…sleeping.

Saturday morning, I woke up. My body was weak and in excruciating pain. Any simple movement felt as though millions of needles were piercing my flesh all at the same time. Suffice to say, as I limbed to the bathroom that morning, I wished the bathroom could somehow magically come to me. Reaching the bathroom, I looked in the mirror and was unprepared to see my face and neck swollen. And not only swollen but full of mucous lesions around my nose, eyes and mouth. The three circular red marks on my chest had multiplied and spread to my neck and arms. Please hear me…the marks inflamed my skin; it felt like a pulsating fire. *Just for a split-second, I thought I was having a nightmare so I closed my eyes and counted to ten but when I opened my eyes, the painful reality remained.* I screamed to my daughter in her room, "Cece, I have to get to the hospital". As we bolted to the hospital, I tried to take the attention off of my pain and instructed my daughter to contact family members about my condition and attempted to arrange plans to transport my daughter back to Kentucky State University for the Spring semester – but my daughter was not adhering to the latter.

I don't remember how I got into the emergency room – but within minutes nurses wearing protective masks were scurrying around me connecting intravenous fluids, checking my vitals and inquiring of myself and my daughter of any recent international trips, current medications, interactions with medically symptomatic individuals and family history and health conditions. Next, a series of blood work was ordered and drawn for testing from my inflamed arms as the red marks continued to shuffle down my body…etching towards my stomach. *Talk about excruciating pain!!* Doctors in the ER, distinctly dressed in their spring white coats, looked completely baffled. Of the four doctors consulting on my case, only one doctor confessed in humility and with human compassion that they were unsure of my medication condition. However, he assured me that they are fervently researching my symptoms in medical references and communicating with specialist colleagues. A few moments went by…then I overheard another one of the doctors saying, "*The Center for Disease Control has been notified and is in route. We have to move her to the 6th floor – isolation immediately*". My eyes filled up with tears. I felt a flood of emotions, looking in the corner of the room at my daughter sitting – her marble eyes were piercing every movement in the room. Thoughts of dying captured my mind. I could not speak. Fear of the thought of dying paralyzed my mouth. I began to scream within my spirit. Tears saturated the mucous lesions on my face. Medical professionals rushed me speedily down the hallway, round a corner and up to the 6th floor via a side elevator. My room was quarantined. A plastic insulated chamber with a big burnt orange caution warning, notifying everyone to enter with protective garments. Everyone adhered except my daughter. She was fearless. At this point, my mind started racing again on thoughts of dying but I looked across the room at my daughter's courage and I knew I had to fight. This pain. This suffering. This dis-ease was serious. In my spirit, I began a choral utterance, "I shall not die, but live..." (Psalm 118:17). Seconds later, nurses rushed in the room to administer medicine to ease the pain and induce sleep. I quickly informed my daughter of a list of needed items and garments from home as the fluids ran through the IV. For me, any relief from the pain is welcomed medicine.

Sunday. I was awake. I knew this fact because my body and mind were alert – but the darkness which prevailed was disturbing. My eyes were 'wide shut'. Another symptom of this dis-ease. As I raised my hands to pry my eyelids open, I heard footsteps in my chamber, a female nurse had entered. She had a pleasant demeanor and voice. I explained the condition of my eyes – and she proceeded to apply a warm cleansing cloth to the eye area and assisted me to pry open my eyelids. Momentarily, walking into the room without protective garments, my daughter arrived, carrying all the items and garments on my list, just in time to help me shower and apply my purple silk head wrap. Attempts to eat had been fruitless because the mucous lesions were encapsulated the interior walls of my mouth. I could only drink cold liquids. Throughout the day, doctors came, looked at my condition and the spreading red lesions on my skin but no diagnosis was offered. Nurses visited on ordered hourly intervals to draw my blood but no indication was noted about my condition. Everyone was silent. *I do believe the medical professionals were doing everything within the scope of their knowledge but I was in so much pain – and becoming catatonic furious with all of the poking from the beehive of medical professionals without receiving a diagnosis.*

By Tuesday; Day 4, my eyes were fused together. Prying was not a viable option. I could only sit and allow my other senses to become dominant. Again, I was awake, lying in bed and heard footsteps entering my chambers. I simply remained silent and still. Judging from the smell of the cologne, it was a man. The sound of the footsteps informed me that it was more than one man. Low voice conversation initiated. The doctors were discussing my case. They noted all of my blood work was screened and tested for a gamut of diseases and viral infections but all of the results were negative. They noted that the current intravenous antibiotic is not preventing the ailment from spreading – and should the condition continue to spread at such a rapid pace, I would not make it to the end of the day. I began my chorale utterance again within my spirit, "I shall not die… but live". However, my utterance erupted verbally. The doctors went completely silent. After a brief pause, one doctor asked, '*How are you feeling today?*'. My reply was short with a probing question as to what are the next steps since all of my tests were negative. I wanted (no I needed) to know if what I overheard about 'not making it to the end of the day' was accurate. I waited patiently for a response. The silence in the chamber was deafening – and interrupted by an entering click-click shoe heel. I know a woman had entered the chamber – but *WHO?*

The collegial introductions answered my question. It was a local female dermatologist who specializes in internal medicine. Opening my hospital gown (*I was clothed with my gown opening in the front*), I felt her feminine hands examining the red lesions on my stomach and legs. Leaning me forward with gentle assistance, acknowledging my pain and discomfort, she also examined the marks on my back – and immediately spoke healing words to shift the gridlock of medical quandary, "*It's Stevens Johnson. Reviewing her chart, she had to have had an allergic reaction to some form of medication administered to her prior to entering the hospital...she is not contagious...release the isolation...I will be administering a new medication....stop that current IV antibiotic it is making the illness worse...*". My heart was immediately filled with joy. *But who was Stevens Johnson? I never asked to meet him.* I grabbed the hand of the female dermatologist, asking her if she was absolute about this diagnosis. She replied yes. Before I allowed my emotions to further mount with appreciation, as I finally received a diagnosis, I inquired about my eyes, explaining that I have been in the darkness for three days. With a clam and assertive tone, she informed me that Stevens Johnson Syndrome is a toxic life-threatening condition; a hypersensitivity complex in which cell death causes the epidermis to separate from the dermis, affecting the skin and the mucous membranes, causing conjunctivitis (inflammation of eyes and eyelids) and mucosal desquamation (ulcers and lesions in the mouth reducing ability to eat and drink). Continuing to provide me with condensed facts of the diagnosis and recovery process, this kind female dermatologist whose face I was unable to see, informed me that a licensed ophthalmologist specializing in corneal and refractive surgery and external eye disease will be here this afternoon to consult on my case – and conduct surgery if deemed necessary. THIS moment was poignant. I had received a diagnosis and a second chance....regardless of my eyes being 'wide shut'.

The ophthalmologist arrived approximately one hour after my transition to Room 629. His footsteps were heavy like his voice. He was not as gentle as the female dermatologist. He seemed hurried – so I candidly expressed my appreciation for his medical consult on my case but kindly insisted on a milder manner on the examination of my eyes as my threshold for pain was maxed. The next touch on my eyelid was firm but milder. *I could live with that.* At the conclusion of his examination, he explained to me that Stevens Johnson syndrome frequently causes the formation of scar tissue inside of the eyelids, leading to corneal vascularization, impaired vision and a host of other ocular problems. The good news, he continued, is that miraculously you have no scarring in your eye wall. However, two ocular insertions are required for scar and permanent damage prevention. I cannot express in words the pain and pressure associated with this ophthalmologic insertion. *However, I do extend my sincere gratitude to all of the medical professionals who acted as human body restraints, holding my head, hands and body firmly in place during this procedure.* This was a moment of sweet relief. With my recovery ocular inserts, it was my pleasure to see and express my appreciation to the ophthalmologist for his consult and 'steady hand' procedure which instantly transformed my situation out of the darkness and into the light.

Within two days, the circular red rash of lesions about an inch on my face, neck, arms, legs, scalp and soles of my feet, though still painful, stopped spreading. The new medication was effective. It was targeting the root cause of the illness and providing evidence of healing. In that moment, it did not occur to me nor did it matter to me that I would still spend two more weeks in the hospital undergoing a series of further blood work including insulin shots; that my taste buds would not be functional for months; that my hair would fall out because of the lesions scars in my scalp; that I would completely deplete my savings and max-out all of my credit cards paying for ER medical, post discharge and recovery medical expenses exceeding $26,000; that I would have to initially follow-up with eight physician specialists post discharge; that my recovery would be a lonely process as my family members and loved ones were unable to travel to Louisville to be with me during this crisis; that it would be months before I would be physically able to return to my career; that it would be more than three years before my skin condition normalizes; that my skin would be permanently scarred as a reminder of my intimate meeting with Stevens Johnson. Nope, I did not give any thought to these things. I was too grateful to allow this *kairos* moment to pass by…I had to offer prayer and thanksgiving to God.

BIRTHDAY BUTTERFLY WINGS

February 7th 2011. My Orlando, Florida birthday celebration was aborted. I was 40, recently discharged from the hospital, sitting on my deep brown chaise lounge crying and listening to Bishop TD Jakes. I cannot recall the title of his message. My journal writing reflects that Bishop TD Jakes stated the following:

> *"The sound of birthing is always crying…You've got internally inside of you all that you need. The strength on the inside needs to manifest into strength on the outside…You've got to EMERGE!....Out of the Cocoon into a Butterfly…"*

As Bishop Jakes continued his message, I continued to cry, weeping as the phrase, "**EMERGE!**..out of the cocoon into a butterfly" echoed over and over again in my spirit. In this moment, I realized the butterfly effect of my Stevens Johnson encounter.

Abbreviating the process, the metamorphosis of a butterfly entails four cyclic stages: **egg, larva** (the feeding stage), **pupa** (the transitioning stage) and **adult** (the reproductive stage). Every butterfly begins its life as an EGG. When a butterfly larva (also known as a caterpillar) first hatches from its egg; it is very small. *A caterpillar has only one job: to eat!* Caterpillars can grow 100 times their size during the larva stage- and faces a peculiar challenge as they grow because their skin cannot grow with them. In order for a caterpillar to grow larger than the skin it had when it hatched, it must make a new, larger skin. The caterpillar does this by first growing a new skin underneath the outer skin. Then, when it is ready, it 'sheds' the old skin and the newer, larger skin underneath is exposed. This process is properly called molting – and a caterpillar can molt about 4 or 5 times. When the caterpillar molts for the fifth and final time, the new skin underneath forms the outer shell of the chrysalis. The chrysalis (generally referred to as a pupa) is not a "resting" stage as many people think. The pupa may be suspended under a branch, hidden in leaves or buried underground – but contrary to public opinion, a lot is happening to the pupa. It may not look like nothing is going on but big changes (transformation) are happening on the inside. The body of the caterpillar is transforming into an adult butterfly. Special cells that were present in the larva are now growing rapidly becoming legs, wings and eyes. Antennae are formed and the chewing mouthparts of the caterpillar are transformed into the sucking mouthparts of the butterfly. The pupa stage can last from a few weeks, a month or even longer until it is ready to

EMERGE into a butterfly. *WOW! ,in personal reflection,* Guess what? *I had a butterfly effect. I've grown in my affliction; shed my old caterpillar skin and transformed into a BUTTERFLY!!! I had to exercise my flight muscles – but the essence (strength) on inside of me is now radiating on the outside. I have BEAUTIFUL Butterfly Wings. Well, Happy 40ᵗʰ Birthday to me!!!!* Perception is always imperative as we encounter challenging and defining moments. I like how Susan L. Taylor captures the purpose of life's journey in her book ***Lessons in Living***, **"There are no meaningless experiences. Every interaction, every event along our journey has significance, because it shapes how we perceive ourselves and how we view life. Rather than simply responding emotionally to a challenge, we must practice looking within ourselves to discover the meaning of our experiences. The key is our ability to pause – to put aside our egos and suspend judgment long enough to allow that still, small voice within to be heard. Once we make that mental shift, we can begin to view our lives from a higher perspective. The truth is that everything – a lover's betrayal, a parent's harsh remark, even a health challenge - is a lesson for our growth, not for our oppression. Our lives become a painful journey only when we resist, rather than accept, the lessons on our path that are God's invitation to grow"**.

Much of what I do at EMERGE, PLLC is about equipping individuals to live fuller, more productive lives. Our company slogan is "A different harvest requires a different seed". The key to change begins in our thought processes. Thoughts are powerful. Thoughts are the prelude to action/behavior. You think it; then you do it. When we continue thinking in the same old way – we can't expect to achieve different results or produce different behaviors. If you want a different harvest, you have to plant a different seed. My Intimate Meeting with

Stevens Johnson, though uninvited, was a thought provoker of the Divine kind. During my illness, like most people, I asked God why I had to go through such a terrible medical crisis – but I received no answer. Today, three and a half years later, as I write these final words, I believe my meeting with Stevens Johnson ushered me into exactly what I wanted for this decade in life: a self-loving transitional season. My life before Stevens Johnson and after this defining moment is completely different. I praise God for seeing me through my meeting with Stevens Johnson and giving me a whole new way of thinking. I have a deeper sense of gratitude for myself; the created purpose and essence that makes me authentically Charmaine – and I love it!!!! *Trust me, I don't understand why Stevens Johnson stopped by to introduce himself to me. I am as baffled as the medical professionals - but I trust that if God allowed it – in some way or form it will work for my amazing good.*

The last page of 'O' Magazine always features Oprah Winfrey's *What I know for Sure* reflections. Allow me to answer. What I know for sure is I did not die in my affliction.... ***God snatched my life Out of the Darkness, Into the Light – and for this I am forever GRATEFUL.***

Suggested Readings
Holy Bible – Psalms 91

Lessons in Living by *Susan L. Taylor*

Healed without Scars by *David G. Evans*

Living Through the Meantime by *Iyanla Vanzant*

Showing Mary by *Renita J. Weems*

Thrive: 7 Strategies for Extraordinary Living by *Felicia T. Scott*

Notes:

_____

_____

_____

_____

_____

_____

_____

_____

_____

_____

_____

_____

_____

_____

_____

_____

_____

_____

_____

ABOUT THE AUTHOR

CHARIS BROWN

Charis Brown is the founder of Healing Grace LLC, a nonprofit organization focused on divorce recovery for women. The organization facilitates retreats, workshops, coaching, and counseling sessions for women who have encounter divorce. The goal of the organization is to guide divorced women towards their individual healing and restoration thru Jesus Christ. Ms. Charis started the organization in 2013 a year after her second divorce. Her passion is to speak truth to women who suffer from the lies and confusion that can consume them after a divorce. Charis once believed the lies and confusion after her divorce and it took her down a dark path that she wants no other women to endure.

In addition Charis is a certified Women's Leadership Coach who specializes in women's empowerment, confidence building, and professionalism. Ms. Charis is a member of The American Association of Christian Counselors and Extraordinary Women Ministries.

Charis currently lives in KY with her two amazing daughters and is pursuing a Bachelor's Degree in Women's Ministry. When she is not studying or working as a clinical specialist, you can find her writing, reading, travelling, enjoying watching her oldest daughter run track and her youngest daughter marching in the band. However more than any of the accomplishments listed above Charis's most satisfying accomplishment is the personal relationship she has with her Lord and Savior Jesus Christ.

Contact:
Charis Brown
Healing Grace LLC
Email: healinggracedivorcerecovery@gmail.com
Facebook: Healing Grace Divorce Recovery for Women
Phone: 502-352-0244

SEVEN

A Hidden Rift

Charis Brown

"O Lord, you have examined my heart and know everything about me. You know when I sit down and stand up. You know my thoughts even when I'm far away. You see me when I travel and when I rest at home. You know everything I do. You know what I am going to say even before I say it, Lord. You go before me and follow me. You place your hand of blessing on my head. Such knowledge is too wonderful for me, too great for me to understand! I can never escape from your Spirit! I can never get away from your presence! If I go up to heaven, you are there; if I go down to the grave, you are there If I ride the wings of the morning, if I dwell by the farthest oceans, even there your hand will guide me, and your strength will support me". Psalm 139 vs. 1-10.

What a relationship to have that you can choose a path where no matter what you have Christ's love, support, and guidance. Imagine the lover of your soul saying I'm here no matter the circumstance if you mess up I will show you the correct path. Well unfortunately for me when I encountered my second divorce this scripture was foreign to me. The circumstances and lies that the enemy wanted me to believe cause a hidden rift between me and my relationship with Christ. These lies seemed to be true because they were not bold or extreme, no they were ever so quiet even gift wrapped with a bow. They seemed completely rationale and beneficial to me. The lies traveled down to the core of my heart and stayed there continuously working to pull me further away from truth. Scripture says in 1 Corinthians 14:33 "For God is not a God of confusion but of peace". So let me share with you some of the lies and confusion I believed after I divorced, and why these lies were such a contradiction to the truth.

"John 8:44 you are of your father the devil, and your will is to do your father's desires. He was a murderer from the beginning, and does not stand in the truth, because there is no truth in him. When he lies, he speaks out of his own character, for he is a liar and the father of lies."

I have come to learn through experience that the enemy wants to attack when we are broken to Steal our Joy, kill the truth, and destroy our lives. When I was attacked while broken the enemy came to steal, kill, and destroy all that I had. It is an eye opener now when I look back and can see now how I was so quick to assume or complain about what I believed God wasn't doing. Hardly ever did I pay attention to what God was doing or what the enemy was trying to do in my life. In my case the enemy brought lies and total confusion to my door step. I had many but to narrow it down here is the list of the top five lies and before confusion I believed.

1. I'm a failure and life isn't worth living anymore

2. I can't show weakness I must bounce back

3. I need a man to fill the void of loneliness in my heart and to move forward

4. It must be my physical appearance that caused my failed marriages

5. Its ok to hold hatred and un forgiveness in my heart

These five lies robbed my healing, attacked my deliverance and tried to steal my testimony. The lies also stole my self-esteem, killed my joy, and attempted to destroy my life. The five examples listed above are actually five different testimonies of how my personal relationship with Christ was deepened and they were all just waiting to be shared and the enemy knew this. There are testimonies that may help someone else come through to see truth instead of believing the lie. I have come to learn, if a testimony is shared it brings forth truth and light. Testimonies also have the power to become contagious they guide us toward our own path of healing, deliverance, and they have the ability to help others along the way. The lies the enemy plants in us places a wall in front of our testimonies. If a testimony can be blocked it can negatively impact the same people it was originally intended to bless. With the lies growing and my belief in them, I noticed my decisions were clouded and eventually my path was blocked. Interestingly enough this all occurred precisely at the time when Jesus wanted to begin the process of healing the brokenness within my heart.

I'm a failure and life isn't worth living anymore

It was a cold day in December 2011 when my second husband walked out of me and the kid's life. It was sudden and not expected at all. When he left it was so unexpected that thirty days prior we went on our second year anniversary getaway. I was speechless and a bunch of questions hit me at the same time. What happened because as far as I knew our marriage wasn't perfect but nothing was so bad that either of us would just walk away? How do I tell the kids? What did I do? Was it me? It was during this time I hit my lowest point in life. I let my second failed marriage dictate my identity as a failure in life. I told myself I must have failed miserably because I had no idea my husband would just up and leave, what kind of wife am I? Nothing for me at this point mattered as much as being a good wife and mother. I had no other identity all I ever wanted stemmed from my husband and kids. I even lost my desire to have a relationship with Christ. I told myself I knew Jesus and I was a believer so that was good enough. My focus was entirely on my husband at this point and trying to figure out what I would do, since he is gone with no explanation or warning. I felt as if I was grieving the death of a spouse but my spouse wasn't deceased. The man I spent 6yrs with sharing dreams, plans, and our family desires just disappeared. This state of confusion consumed me until I was sinking faster than I could swim. The lie I believed at this point told me that my only way out was taking my life. Yes I was planning my suicide because I felt I had no purpose anymore. The only thing that did make sense was that I was a failure and I was not a good example for my two daughters. I'm a failure and I can't even tell you how I failed, so who can I help when I can't even help myself? I'm damaged goods and worse of all God must not love me anymore; God is punishing me for something but I have no idea what I did. Then it seemed as if people and time were just passing me by. Every waking moment I felt as if no one was there to console me not even to say "I feel your pain". I believed the lie that if I wasn't here anymore it would all be over. No more pain no more issues it's done. Unfortunately, when you believe a lie nothing rational makes sense anymore. That's when you have believed the lies to the point where you feel there is only one path to travel and you are the only one who will travel that road alone.

My First hidden rift was my inability to recognize truth because of the confusion caused by the lie. The lie I believed is that I was in this all alone and my failures yielded me no reason to exist. Scripture spoke truth however in <u>Deuteronomy</u> 31:6 "So be strong and courageous! Do not be afraid and do not panic before them. For the Lord your God will personally go ahead of you. He will neither fail you nor abandon you."

I can't show weakness I must bounce back

My second marriage came upon the heels of my first divorce. When my first marriage ended I was devastated. We were young and listened to everyone and anyone's advice which ultimately led to the advice given to us to just get a divorce. I was even told before the ink was dry on the divorce decree, I needed to date and this led to a second marriage shortly after. Everyone around me told me that was what I needed to do. Yes I can grieve but get over it be a victor not a victim. To get over the hurt and the pain I needed to just move on. Some would also tell me the quicker I did this the faster I would heal. So as a result I decided my goal in my second marriage was to make it as perfect as possible. Fix what I did wrong the first time so that this would never happen again. At least that was the lie that I believed. Get someone else, correct your mistakes, move on and get over it. Well unfortunately I did not realize that that lies right there pulled me further from the love of Christ by setting unrealistic expectations on myself. None of us are perfect and in believing that I was perfect or can obtain perfection was totally missing out on any spiritual growth that God had for me. In setting perfection in self or a relationship I was saying I myself do not need Jesus if all is perfect what can Jesus do for me? Now I didn't walk around saying this out loud. No I was the one that would tell anyone in a heartbeat Jesus Christ is my Lord and savior and I depend on Jesus for everything, while my actions were totally opposite. When Jesus looked at my heart the words didn't matter my actions spoke louder. The enemy endorsed this with what appears to be the perfect marriage, jobs, kids, and lives. I once again did not look at Scripture which clearly states in Psalm 44: 21 "would not God have discovered it, since he knows the secrets of the heart?"

I remember seeing a friend post beautiful pictures of what looked to be an awesome vacation she took on Facebook. When I called to get details she said to me "Charis it was the worst vacation ever. They lost my luggage, my room was not ready and I ate something I was allergic to". After we laughed about it I got off the phone and thought wow, looking at this awesome picture is such an illusion. Then I looked at myself and said wow, my life is the same an illusion. On the outside I looked great a woman who has overcame 2 divorces and is working to get on her feet. However that wasn't the case at all that was my invisible rift. This is where the enemy came in and stole my joy from within. My ability to hide my pain grew stronger day by day. Just as my joy and healing were draining right out of my life. The lie grew bigger and I grew more distant. I remember feeling so numb one day when a friend of mine said "Charis I don't know how you can do it you are a strong woman, to God be the glory". Yes I felt like I finally made it I was a strong woman who needed no one. I had overcome with my own strength and was progressing forward on my own. Everything on the outside was looking great, single mother of 2 who lost everything now has a new home, new car, great job, enrolled back in college and making straight A's. I was strong now and I showed no sign of weakness. At least that's the lie I wanted to believe. With all these perfect things going on in my life, I felt like the vacation my friend took. This was the worst I had ever felt in my life but I appeared to be strong and even better than before. When in reality I felt weak and trapped in a sound proof box screaming but no one could hear me. It was in this box that I felt vulnerable, weak, and hopeless.

My 2nd rift was my ability to look perfect on the outside but I was dying on the inside.

If the enemy can come in and place doubt then life circumstances can consume you and cause you to sink. However there is the truth in God's word which will take you from believing the lie into knowing and trusting In God's truth. 2 <u>Corinthians</u> 12:9 "My grace is sufficient for you, for my power is made perfect in weakness."

I need a man to fill the void of loneliness in my heart

After my second divorce I dated to replace now my first and second husbands. That was not my intention but in truth that was exactly what I was doing. I had two men in my life for 13 yrs. I was the woman who had never been without a male partner since the age of 16 which was half my life, and now I'm divorced at the age of 32 and I didn't know who I was. So naturally when I divorced I panicked. I was lonely, I felt lost, no husband to guide my home, and no one to share my life with. So I dated the following month after the second divorce decree came. I know you're probably reading this and saying to yourself "Charis really you didn't catch on the first time?" No I didn't I'm a hard headed girl as my mother would say. None of the truth mattered I was lonely so this was my remedy for that, at least I thought. This unknowingly to me was an opportunity for the enemy to step in and once again bring more confusion that would pull me further from my healing. I was so overwhelmed by all the men that came out of the woodworks right when I was divorced and lonely. I thought wow this dating thing isn't bad there are tons of guys out there maybe one is my husband. I was so naive when it came to dating but I learned very quickly a lot of these same men had issues worse than mine. As for the other they could recognize that my brokenness was written all over me. In other words I wasn't at all selective in who was in my space. I used no discernment into the choices I was making either. So I got just what I accepted any and everything. I was a fresh fish and I threw myself in a shark tank. Broken, hurt, and confused, I was ready to swim away with whoever said the right thing to me. This went along for a year then after frustrating one day in April I said to myself, I'm done trying this is not working, God help me. I decided to say no thank you I'm not dating now. I closed the door to man and opened the door to God. Yes having someone does feel good in the moment but after the fact you feel worse than before.

Well that's sort of what I said. Let me be honest with you I began reading scripture more and more daily after this because I was determined that I could do it on my own but I would allow God to help some with the loneliness part if need be. I was never really open to tell anyone I read scripture every day because that meant I wasn't perfect or self-sufficient as I appeared. However, as I read I noticed scripture was contradicting my life so much I was actually getting angry. I was angry with God and I would say God really? I mean my life isn't perfect, it's good, and yes it could be a little better so just fix me a little. Send me a God fearing man so I won't be hurt by him and

I can move on, and I will be back on track. That's it God that's all I need from you because I earned that from you. I was a pretty good wife plus you let women who are terrible to their husbands have and keep good men. That's all I need from you God thank you very much and amen. I think to myself now how I must have tickled my God when I prayed that prayer. I still to this day can't believe I was actually telling God how I needed the job to be done. As I look back I tend to get embarrassed and still to this day I check myself and say to myself "wow now that was lunatic bold". In one of my ah ha moments I was able to picture myself as a piece of art that was broken back then. I actually went to the artist and said "look now I don't have time for fixing anything I'm good just slap some paint on me and I will be ok", that's just ridiculous if you think about it. But I can safely say I'm probably not the only woman in this world who has done this.

My third hidden rift was my obsession of seeking a man for healing when Jesus was seeking to heal me. God's word says in Psalm 147:3 "He heals the brokenhearted and binds up their wounds."

My physical appearance that caused my failed marriages

Here it is the hardest one of all for me. The day I learned why my second husband left me. I attributed his decisions and actions to my physical appearance. This happened to be my weight and physical features. I believed the lie that I was too fat and ugly so that's why I'm alone now. I mean that explains it because I can't explain his actions so it must have been me. If I would have eaten less and maybe wore makeup I would have my husband right now. Maybe I needed a complete makeover. I could grow my hair more since he loved long hair and try to loose 100 lbs. That was it I told myself and I did that and guess what it didn't work. The reason this wouldn't work is because I wasn't listening to the truth. The truth was yes I could have made changes but no matter what change I made my second husband made his decision and I needed to accept that his decision to leave was his choice not mine. That is just like someone saying well I don't like you Charis. There is nothing wrong with that because not everyone will like me. However what is wrong with that is if I decided to change who I am to be liked by this person. Now I know it seems that it's not that simple. I have had countless friends tell me well Charis you don't know the circumstances or reasons. Thankfully I don't need to just as I never got a clear truthful reason for why my second husband left me in the beginning. That doesn't matter what does matter is what do I need to overcome this circumstance. We live in a broken fallen world and unfortunately tragic deaths, hatred, and unhappiness is unavoidable. This also includes divorce it happens, it's a reality. I do not believe that God had divorce in his plan any more than unhappiness or hatred however; I have seen what God can do with the circumstance of unhappiness, hatred, and yes divorce. I have seen and heard the testimonies of healing, joy, and restoration in lives that have been impacted by hurtful circumstances.

The enemy found my weakness and my self-esteem was under attack. I had no idea another rift had even started at this point. It's funny how you can get kicked when you're already down and not even know what happened to you. I was hurt by the decision my second husband made however what I am doing to myself as a result of his decision was my own. I remember looking in a mirror even after I lost 100 lbs. and grew all this hair physically I looked better but I was still broken and hurt. The woman in that mirror was not Charis she looked familiar but she wasn't Charis. The reflection in the mirror wasn't who

God created me to be. If I couldn't look in mirror and identify myself then who could? It took me some time to realize God created me uniquely just as he created everyone with their own uniqueness. As a child my mother would always say you are a Divine Original. I thank God for using her to equip me with this knowledge even as a child I was being prepared for a time like this.

My fourth rift was my belief that having control in changing who I was created to be could change the outcome of my past circumstances. Jeremiah 1:5 "Before I formed you in the womb I knew you, and before you were born I consecrated you; I appointed you a prophet to the nations."

It is ok to hold hatred and unforgiveness in my heart

I must say hatred and forgiveness are two forces that no one should ever reckon with. Now of course I had to learn this the hard way. As I told you before I'm very hard headed. Funny I thought I understood this the day my second husband contacted me via email to tell me he was sorry for his actions. I accepted and told him I had forgiven him however, I was really confused still no explanation and no closure at that point. I was still angry, upset, unhappy, and I had no idea why after I told him he was forgiven. Well the reason I didn't know why was because I never forgave myself. How can I forgive someone when I don't know how to forgive myself? C. S Lewis said it best "To be a Christian means to forgive the inexcusable, because God has forgiven the inexcusable in you". So I forgave him but not myself now what?

As I mentioned earlier I was married twice. My first marriage was to my college sweetheart. We planned a beautiful life together filled with nothing but joy and happiness. By the time we were 22 that went out the door and I went to everyone else but my husband for our marriage. Then it began stress from being married young, two kids that were 15 months apart, finances, time, you name it we experienced it. Unfortunately our marriage ended and I blamed myself for its failure. I sought advice not realizing there is advice that could lead you further away from Gods plans for you as a couple as it did us. We had problems and nothing has changed, so divorce it seemed so clear and simple. So why was it shortly after we separated I started to build such a hatred and unforgiveness in my heart for myself. I mean it was my decision so where was all of this coming from? I decided to ignore it just as if you ignore an infection however, after some point that infection will become toxic and eat away at you. My unforgivness and hatred was what I felt for myself. I couldn't believe how easy it was to forgive someone else who hurt me terribly and how difficult it was to forgive myself. From that day forward I became toxic because I shut down the ability to let love operate freely in my life. I progressed into a second marriage and carried this toxicity within me. I now know and understand God is love and when I shut out love I shut out God in my life. It was not the circumstance of the divorce itself. It was my reaction to the circumstance of the divorce, and as a result I shut out my personal relationship with God.

My 5th Hidden rift was when I said I will never forgive myself for my actions. The actual moment I shut God totally out of my life. Luke 7:47-48 " I tell you, her sins, and they are many, have been forgiven, so she has shown me much love. But a person who has forgiven little shows only little love." Then Jesus said to the woman, "Your sins are forgiven".

I pray that you are able to see where the enemy is causing you to be confused with lies. There is a process to your healing, just as it is a process to learn how to go from brokenness into all the promises of life that God has for you. I pray that if there is any unforgivness in your heart that you will please ask and allow Jesus Christ to come into your heart and mend it. Know that unforgivness doesn't disappear on its own overnight. Forgiveness when truly experienced is a blessing beyond belief. When you forgive you are able to see clearly how the enemy will try to keep you stuck in your past. If you stay in the past you will not see all the blessings that God has for you in the present.

ABOUT THE AUTHOR

REGINA BANKS-HALL

Regina Banks-Hall: Business Strategist, International Author, Entrepreneur, Personal and Professional Mentor. Regina is a gifted speaker and motivator, inspiring women of all ages to fulfill their destiny using their God-given talent.

Regina possesses a keen business acumen, developing strategies to improve business operations, employee training and development, and overall organization efficiency, working for retail, automotive and local government industries. Regina operates an online promotional product business, assisting businesses both large and small with their marketing efforts. For the past four years, she has served as a freelance writer for the Detroit Women's Business Examiner, covering the latest business trends, strategies, and innovations of interest for female business owners.

In addition, Regina works as a volunteer financial coach for her local church. In this role, she meets one-on-one with couples or individuals helping them with personal financial budgeting. Regina is the owner of Regina's All-Star Apparel & Accessories, a promotional products company. She has recently launched a professional development organization, the RBH Professional Development Institute, which offers training, coaching, motivational and inspirational material for women and teens.

Regina is a two time Baker College Alumni, holding a BA in Business Management and a MBA in Human Resource Management. Regina is currently enrolled in a DBA Program at Walden University, specializing in Leadership, Strategy and Innovation. Regina is a member of the Professional Woman Network (PWN), Society of Human Resource Management (SHRM), American Society of Training and Development (ASTD), National Association of Professional Women (NAPW), American Management Association (AMA), the Black MBA Association (BMBAA) and Toastmasters International.

Regina believes her purpose is to inspire women to overcome their fear and walk into their destiny.

Books:

Co-Author: The Confident Woman: Tapping Into Your Inner Power
Co-Author: The Female Leader: Empowerment, Confidence & Passion
Co- Author: Second Chance Living: Out of the Darkness, Into the Light

Expertise:

Talent Management
Strategic Management
Professional Coaching & Mentorship
Personal Coaching & Mentorship
Human Resource Management
Promotional Marketing Specialist

Contact:
Regina Banks-Hall, MBA
Redford Township, Michigan
Telephone (866) 600-6322
Fax (866) 505-2287
Email rbankshall@gmail.com
Websites: www.regina-gifts.com   www.rbankshall.com
Blogger for Detroit Women's Business Examiner
http://www.examiner.com/womens-business-1-in-detroit/regina-banks-hall

EIGHT

It is Time to Walk Into Your Greatness

Regina Banks-Hall

"I am here to change the world with small acts of kindnesses, realizing that my small attempt to empower everyone supports the greater good"
—Regina Banks-Hall

It was a cold November night in 2008. I was at home washing a turkey getting ready for my Thanksgiving dinner and the telephone rang. It was Kelly Automotive Services, calling to tell me my contract assignment with Chrysler was ending. I hung up the phone, shared the news with my husband, and went back into the kitchen. The following Monday, I would file for unemployment for the first time in my life. Over the next few weeks, the shock would turn into anger.

I could not believe I was unemployed. I survived Thanksgiving and Christmas and began the New Year, with the reality of collecting unemployment insurance.

One day, after collecting unemployment insurance for several months, I realized God had given me a second chance for success. However, in order to embrace the opportunity, I had to end my pity party, and get out of the bed. I was reminded of my favorite scripture, which states, "I can do all things through Christ which strengthens me" (Philippians 4.13). A few weeks later, I received a letter to attend a meeting regarding a program helping individuals interested in finishing their education or earning an advanced degree. I learned that I qualified for a program that would allow me the opportunity to go back to school. I enrolled and went back to school earning my MBA, and by the end of this year my DBA.

Also, during this period of personal development, I was focused on generating some new experiences. As I began settle into my new life, I began to find a purpose in what I was doing. I was working as a substitute teacher, volunteering time as a budget counselor for my church and going to school. I was also helping my family by attending to the needs of my father-in-law who was ill. I was beginning to see a future for myself, and finding joy in how God was using my gifts and talents.

One day while I was working in an elementary school, breaking up a fight, I felt the vibration of my cell phone. After checking the message, someone was calling me with a job offer. I jumped at the opportunity and three years later, I am now managing that department. As I began to make changes personally and professionally, I began to grow and develop as an individual. Now as I evaluate the last six years of my life, I have discovered that, hope, optimism, passion, positive relationships, good habits, loving myself, and taking control of my life, were the keys to my success.

As I began to focus on this chapter, it occurred to me, that God altered my comfortable environment with some adversity in order for me to find my purpose, and walk into my greatness. Now that I am on my new journey, I want to share with you 7 steps for walking into your greatness, and receiving a second chance for living, walking out of the darkness into the light.

The seven steps are as follows:

1. Take control over your life

2. Become hopeful

3. Create good habits

4. Develop a positive relationship with yourself.

5. Find your passion

6. Expand your network and build your relationships

7. Visualize the future

In order to walk into your greatness, we must all begin the journey, by taking control over our lives. We can take the first step, when we accept the responsibility that we can alter our journey, even in the mist of adversity. Through my own personal journey, I noticed that women struggle to move ahead, because they are afraid of their prior mistakes. They are also afraid of what other people will say about their new direction, progress, or the changes they are making. The important lesson in this example is to understand that everyone makes mistakes, and we are all works in progress striving for perfection. Our goal is to learn from our mistakes and move forward.

In addition, when you take control over your life, you set yourself free from the embarrassment associated with the mistakes and experiences of your past. This freedom is also associated with forgiveness, and it opens the door towards accepting the possibilities associated with your future. Another favorite scripture of mine states, "God has not given us the spirit of fear, but of power, love and a sound mind (2 Timothy 1:7). As you take control over your life, address the fears you have about success. Know that you have the power within you to start over, and only you stand in the way of achieving success.

Now take a moment to list some things that are holding you back, and as you identify these obstacles, think about how you will overcome them with what you have learned from this chapter.

_____

_____

_____

_____

_____

_____

The second step towards walking into your greatness is finding hope. Hope by definition, promotes the desire of a positive outcome. Hope is an optimistic attitude because you can expect with confidence that your situation will improve and change. A key part of hope is associated with the belief that, as individuals we have the power to change our circumstances. When I became unemployed, I went through a phase of anger and depression. I began to challenge God, because I believed that I was doing everything the right way. However, after evaluating myself, I identified areas for improvement.

I also realized that God was in control of my life, and as long as I kept my faith in him, nothing could hold me back. I began to say to myself, "No weapon formed against me would prosper (Isaiah 54:17). Over time, my anger and depression would be, removed, and I knew it was time for me to move forward into my purpose. Leviticus 26:4 states "I will give you rain in due season, and the land shall yield her increase and the trees of the field yield their fruit". In due season, it began to rain and the trees I planted began to yield their fruit. As I picked the fruit off the tree, I began to focus on the positive changes in my life, and negative thoughts disappeared.

Now take some time, and determine what areas in your life provide hope for a successful future.

_____

_____

_____

_____

_____

_____

_____

The third step towards walking into your greatness requires you to create good habits. Creating good habits can benefit many areas of your life. Some good habits I have currently implemented include daily exercise, reading and relaxation. Some other great suggestions would be, save 10% of your income, do not be on time, be early, and finally, set aside time for your spiritual life. It is also important to create balance, spending quality time with family and friends. Every year for our anniversary, my husband and I have a little hideaway we will visit in Northern Michigan. At this hideaway, we can play golf, walk along the pier, go fishing, and this year I am going horseback riding. This trip allows us to spend quality time together, which relieves much stress and tension.

Finally, developing and maintaining a positive attitude can serve as the best medicine for walking into your greatness. Philippians 4:8 states, "Finally, whatever is true, whatever is noble, whatever is right, whatever is pure, whatever is lovely, whatever is admirable, if anything is excellent or praiseworthy, think on these things." Finally, the best habit is to select several positive actions, and make them a part of your daily routine.

Now take a moment and assess what good habits you currently possess. After reading this chapter, what good habits do you think you might add?

_____

_____

_____

_____

_____

_____

_____

The fourth step requires you have a good relationship with yourself. In order to move forward and walk into your greatness, you must have a successful relationship with "you." This requires that you change how you view yourself, your current situation, and your future. When you stand in front of a mirror, what do you think of yourself? Do you use degrading words to describe yourself? Do you allow others to define you? Are you at peace with your size, your complexion and your unique personal features, or are you constantly changing yourself to please others?

Well my friend let me lighten your load by telling you that, you are a wonderful creation, full of destiny and purpose. You were designed to make an impact. Our creator designed each of us for our individual purpose, and it is time you walk into your greatness. However, in order to have a good relationship with yourself, you must change the words you use to describe yourself, and change the signals that you emit when you communicate with others. This includes how you walk, how you speak, your attitude and temperament, and how you carry yourself. I always say, walk confidently, speak purposefully, monitor your moods, and carry yourself like the Queen that you are.

Above all, practice removing self-doubt. Therefore, if you become angry and begin to doubt your own ability, state boldly to yourself, that "Greater is He who is in me than he that is in the World (1st John 4:4). Also, refrain from analyzing the darkness of your situation and use powerful words that will bring light and hope. Some of my favorite word choices include, conqueror, victorious, strong, mighty and powerful.

Some additional steps I recommend is to surround yourselves with friends, who will support you in feeling good about yourself. You want to surround yourself with individuals who can help you maintain positive emotions and outlooks. Whenever I need to bounce ideas off someone or discuss my frustrations, I talk to my husband and two of my special girlfriends. Each of these individuals love me enough to tell me the truth, but most importantly, encourage me to move forward.

Second, quiet your mind. Our minds are a wonderful tool for dreams, goals and ambitions, but constant negativity can lead to stress. Add some daily meditation choices such as music, gardening, painting or taking a nature walk. Create an atmosphere where you can focus on the beauty of life. Add nourishment, and eat foods that lead to a healthy mind and body. It is also important to exercise and stay active. Finally, have some fun. I suggest taking up a new sport, a dance class, hanging out with friends, or helping those in need. The goal is to find a way to add some joy to your life.

Now take a moment and think of what you can do to build a better relationship with yourself. As you look back over this chapter, what ideas really stood out to you?

_____

_____

_____

_____

_____

_____

_____

The fifth step requires you find your passion. Determining what you are passionate about is tough and can take time. It starts with how you define the word passion. Passion for me entails feeling excited to be alive, helping others achieve education, encouraging people to use their God given talent and enjoying special moments with family and friends. It is earning my own education, and watching others discover their unique purpose. It is co-authoring this book, and hoping that some other women will discover that it is time to walk into her individual greatness.

I learned that I was not passionate about becoming rich. It was too much work, required too much time, and in the end, God would supply my needs. For example, I have always desired to own my own business. I sold cosmetics, made soap, and operated a tax business. I became frustrated with operating those businesses because they did not

ignite my true inner passion.   I became uninspired, wearing myself
thin trying to keep up with society's version of success.

Eventually I started a screen-printing and embroidery business,
I own today. To date I still own those businesses, however it was not
until I developed a good relationship with myself, that I realized my
true passions were centered on my ability to help others achieve their
goals.   I begun this journey obtaining higher education, co-authoring
motivational books, and creating a non-profit organization, to help
others find their own success. I stopped living according to the
expectation of others, and created my own personal roadmap and my
own definition of success.

**Take a moment and list some things that ignite your passion. How
can you use your passion to help others?**

_____

_____

_____

_____

_____

_____

_____

The sixth step requires you expand your network and build
good relationships. One of the best ways to walk into your greatness
requires that we expand our network and build good relationships.

One important way to expand your network is through volunteerism. Each year, that I am able, I volunteer time with the Susan G. Komen organization. The time allows me to meet cancer survivors, help others, and support a worthwhile cause.

Another great organization is Toastmasters. Toastmasters is an International communication and leadership development organization. The company has over 200,000 members who meet monthly to improve their speaking and leadership skills. I am a member of Toastmasters, and at a recent meeting, I realized that I was sitting in a room with some incredible individuals. Some of us commanded the attention of the room; some of us were fatherly in our conversations, others motherly. Some of us displayed a "DIVA" like mentality while others conducted themselves like CEOs. Although we are different in our abilities and experiences, we share a common bond, because we are all striving to better ourselves bridging together our unique gifts and talents.

Another favorite organization of mine is the Professional Women's Network. This network provides empowerment services for women designed to improve their individual brand through book publishing, training, networking and certification. It is a great forum for growth, personal and professional development, and for some, a second chance for greatness.

Research and or list some organizations you would like to join.

_____

_____

_____

The seventh and final step requires you to visualize your future. As I was recovering from my job loss, I began to visualize my own growth and development. I saw myself as an Author, Doctoral student, Manager and Adjunct faculty member. I maintained a visualization of my goals and dreams on a daily basis, and recited my favorite scriptures to keep myself motivated. As my circumstances begun to change, I began to inspire others through mentorship, positive affirmations, and building my own library of inspirational material. As I began to see myself in a different light, I began to act differently. All of these steps helped to move me in the right direction.

Now as I evaluate the last six years, hope, optimism, passion, positive relationships and good habits have been major keys to my success. As I continue my personal and professional development, I have become an advocate for individuals who believe they cannot make a difference due to their circumstances. We can overcome any obstacle if we believe in our own abilities. As current, future and new leaders, we must never underestimate the power of hope, because it promotes the desire of a positive outcome. Optimism, allows us to expect the best outcome in spite of current events. Passion, starts in our souls and is fueled by what we believe is important in our life. Positive relationships with God, family and friends are the glue that holds us together in tough times. Finally, good habits are the foundation of successful outcomes.

The psalmist David wrote, "Weeping may endure for a night, but joy is coming in the morning" (Psalms 30:5). Therefore, you have every reason to visualize your future. Your dark season will end. Each day you rise should remind you that night is followed by, daylight. It does not matter where you are, it only matters where you finish. King Solomon was, considered by many to be the wisest man in his time. In all of his wisdom, he left on record this encouraging, and thought provoking, statement. "The end of a matter is better than the beginning and patience is better than pride." (Ecclesiastes 7:8).

What do you visualize for your future? What did you read that will encourage you to keep trying?

_____

_____

_____

_____

_____

_____

Your success is within reach, if you can remain hopeful, optimistic, and passionate. Knowing that your positive relationships will give you strength and your good habits will produce a bountiful harvest. You now have a second chance opportunity for living, and it is time you walk into your greatness. Therefore, appreciate what you have, and who you are. When you are comfortable with yourself, you can embrace situations that provide an opportunity for growth.

Additional Reading

8 Reasons Your Life Matters – John Herrick

The 7 habits of Highly Effective People – Stephen R. Covey

Your Words Hold a Miracle – Joel Osteen

Notes:

NINE

In His Hands: Survivor and Conquer

Sheba Harrington

Sheba was raised on the east coast by an upper-middle class African-American family. Her father became a successful entrepreneur early in life, which was a trait passed down from his grandparents. He had numerous business ventures allowing him to give Sheba and her siblings a great childhood. He started in the brick mason industry after high school and quickly moved up in the company from laborer to bricklayer to foreman, and ultimately to partner. Her father's perspective on life was work hard, play hard. During this time he met Sheba's mother and they married.

Shortly after the wedding, Sheba was born. A beautiful baby girl who was very active and full of life. She was always playing, dancing, and getting into everything; but, as in many families, domestic violence existed. This negatively impacted Sheba's childhood and adolescent mental growth. At any time, one day could be peaceful with happiness in the air and the next could be gloomy with arguing and rage.

From the ages of five to eleven Sheba witnessed a great deal of mental, verbal, financial, and physical abuse between both parents. Usually insecurity and adultery were the root causes of a great deal of this dysfunction. Sheba yearned for a loving family where there was peace, love, happiness, laughter, games, commitment, and security; but, this was few and far between.

When Sheba was eleven years old, her parents divorced and her father raised her and her sister. This was a turn for the better in her life because she had security and a home without all the yelling, screaming, and fighting. Sheba's father blessed her with very nice gifts throughout her adolescence. At the age of nine, Sheba had a pony. By eleven she had a horse which she loved. When she turned thirteen she received a trail bike for Christmas. Sheba had to grow up quickly to help run the house. Her father would take Sheba and her sister to the local grocery store and give them money to purchase food and household items. Sheba was responsible for doing most of the cooking. Both sisters cleaned the house and everyone washed clothes, it was a team effort.

Sheba yearned for the happiness of a "normal" family. As with most teenage girls, she became interested in boys and lost interest in the horse and other lovely gifts. She wanted to graduate from high school early; therefore, she went to summer school and graduated by the age of sixteen. She wanted a car for graduation and her father granted her wish, which led to her freedom.

As inherited from her father, Sheba was very charismatic, always winning favor with people. Life for Sheba was fast and furious, full of activity and growth; yet, secretly she always yearned for that loving family unit. Life brought on many blessings and many challenges. Her twenties brought on an unexpected challenge for Sheba which turned her life upside down. After a long battle of cardiac complications and other illnesses, her loving father committed suicide. This changed Sheba's entire life, but God kept her even when she didn't know who He really was.

Sheba developed a personal relationship with God and this changed her life forever. She learned that although she may physically be alone, God was always with her.

Life changing events such as these, will either destroy you or make you stronger. When you have the almighty God on your side, He will carry you through.

Sheba always wanted to get married. She searched high and low for the perfect husband. After years of disappointments, she started praying for her husband. She didn't want to be too demanding so she had a short list. Before you know it he appeared: a tall, dark, handsome, intelligent Christian.

After the two year courtship, they married. Now by this time Sheba was forty and her husband was fifty-six. Yes, Hubbie was a little seasoned, but they were both excited about this new venture.

Two years into their marriage, he was diagnosed with prostate cancer, which effected the romantic connection between these newlyweds. Hubbie went through surgery and two other treatments to remove all cancer, which were successful. The unfortunate part is that their romantic life was tremendously negatively impacted. This stressed Sheba out so badly that she started going into a depression and didn't realize it.

Lesson: 1 in 7 men are diagnosed with prostate cancer

Lesson: Pills don't always work

Lesson: Many women need intimate love, romance, and compassion

Lesson: Numerous romantic opportunities and exciting adventures need to be incorporated into marriage to keep the flame alive.

Quickly the major stress of losing what she always yearned for, a marriage full of love, life, and wonderful romance started taking her down mentally. In addition, her employer started laying off employees quarterly and even laid off multiple people on Sheba's team. Sheba was a hard worker and always received commendations from clients, managers, and co-workers, but she knew that many of the people who had been recently laid off were great employees.

Before Sheba knew it, she started becoming unorganized. It was very difficult for her to keep track of her daily work responsibilities. She was highly stressed, depressed, and overwhelmed. She was on overload and things were spinning out of control. All of a sudden she started feeling majorly depressed because she could not control anything. She was no longer on top of her game. Her mind was not functioning properly and although she was married, she was feeling very lonely. Sheba was so stressed and depressed that she could not sleep.

Lesson: When you are feeling stressed and/or depressed, make sure you talk to someone you can trust about the core of your problems.

Lesson: If you are getting overwhelmed at work, do not wait until you are sick to ask for help. Go to HR and discuss your concerns and request assistance. Some companies have counselors available for their employees.

Lesson: Never cease praying, praising, and attending church.

As time went on, lack of sleep started to weaken Sheba to the point that she was only getting approximately two or three hours of sleep per night. Satan crept in and took this weakness as an opportunity. Sheba's father had given her a beautiful gun as a gift. During one of Sheba's light sleeps, she dreamt of shooting herself, but she thought that it would not be good, because Hubbie would find her and he would be distraught.

The next morning she told her husband about the idea and he immediately took her to see a psychiatrist. The doctor was very concerned and prescribed numerous medications for her to take. Sheba's mind was racing and she just wanted this nightmare to be over. Her life was not what she expected it would be. She did not have the romantic marriage that she had always desired, her relationship with her sisters were strained, her job was in disarray, and she could not turn things around. She felt hopeless.

The next morning Sheba waited until Hubbie left for work. Then she started preparing. She got an extension cord, the prescribed medication, and a knife. It was lightly snowing outdoors, but that did not deter her because she was on a mission to end her life. She was tired of living this unhappy life.

She got in the car and started toward the highway. She drove for about forty-five minutes. Going over long bridges and around corners, looking for a secluded place to hang herself, finally she found a secluded park under a bridge near a boat ramp.

Due to the snow, not many people were out, only a few die-hard fishermen and they were pulling their boats out of the water. Sheba patiently waited for everyone to leave and then she got out of the car.

First, Sheba saw a small bridge and walked over to it, tied the extension cord to one end of the rail and the other end around her neck. She said "Daddy, I'm coming to see you" and jumped over the bridge and fell flat on her behind.

She was so mad at herself, she felt low all over again. She walked around thinking about the next attempt. Suddenly she walked to the edge of the embankment and jumped into the river. The water was cold and deep and, fully clothed, she went under and came up crying out "Lord!". All of a sudden she was swimming back to shore. God was not through with her, for He had great assignments specifically for her.

Quickly she climbed out of the water, mad at herself again. Then, she started pacing back and forth along the embankment looking around. Finally, she slowly walked back to the car, opened the door, and sat inside. She sat there soaking from head to toe, shivering, and thinking about all that had just happened.

She reached for her cell phone and realized that it was in her pocket. Yes, it was full of water and dead. Not good! Her head fell back, trying to get her thoughts together. She remembered that she had another cell phone in her purse which was in the back seat. Sheba reached back and picked up the purse, pulled out the phone, and called her Hubbie. "I'm on my way home. I'll be there in about forty-five minutes." "Are you okay?" he asked. "Yes, I'm fine. I'll be home in about forty-five minutes?" Sheba stated. He gave a sigh of relief. It was a long drive home, the snow was coming down lightly. God's angels protected her all the way home and she arrived safely.

Sheba quickly jumped out of the car, and ran to the front door. She stood there for a minute, then put the key in the door and opened the door. "I'm home", she yelled to her Hubbie who was downstairs.

She quickly stripped off the wet clothes and through them in the washing machine, then ran upstairs to take a nice hot shower. She just knew she was going to catch a cold, if not pneumonia, but God even kept her from getting sick.

Sheba put on her robe and went downstairs where Hubbie stood and started asking questions. First she responded, "I was stressed about the job and all that is going on so I took a ride and went walking by the pond embankment. I accidently fell in, but I'm okay." He looked at her and gave Sheba a big hug and kiss. "I'm glad you are safe and home" he said.." Sheba went into the family room and started watching TV. As she sat there, she couldn't stand the fact that she lied to Hubbie so she told him the truth. "I tried to commit suicide today, but I was not successful. I feel lonely, we have our challenges, the job has been laying people off and I may be next... I am tired of living." They both sat there quietly watching TV, at least Sheba thought he was watching CSI, but he was thinking about how to get Sheba help.

The next morning Sheba woke up and heard Hubbie in his office on the phone talking to someone. He got off the phone and came into the bedroom. "Sheba, get dressed, I am taking you to the doctor", he said softly. Sheba got up, showered, and dressed. They got in the car and off they went.

About twenty long minutes later they arrived at the psychiatrist's office. The office was packed. Hubbie told Sheba to have a seat while he checked in at the front desk. Sheba sat there looking around the room at people who seemed to be looking at her. Quickly Sheba and Hubbie were called to the back.

The psychiatrist and counselors questioned each of them separately and then together for about an hour. Sheba became overwhelmed and started crying and so did Hubbie. Their emotions were out of control, not knowing what the future would hold. All of a sudden, these escorts came and Hubbie stated that it was time to go. Sheba knew something was not right, so she became extremely paranoid.

As they were leaving, people kept staring at them and these escorts acted like she was a villain. Sheba thought she was going to be arrested or something because everyone was acting so strangely. She began to not even trust Hubbie and didn't want to leave the clinic. Finally, they got to the door and she saw a police paddy wagon. Sheba really thought she was being arrested now and she didn't want to go out the door. She quickly turned around and exited to the bathroom down the hall. When she came out Hubbie and the escorts were there. Hubbie took her by the arm and escorted her out the door. Sheba started crying out "NOOOO!". They walked by the paddy wagon and went to the car.

Sheba was out of her mind, literally, and didn't know it. The psychiatrist had given her medicine to calm her, but it had not started working yet. They started driving and Sheba calmed down. All of a sudden the phone rang. Hubbie answered and said, "Hello". Then he got quiet and listened. He then said, "Yes, we are on our way. Oh, okay. You sure? We are about twenty minutes away. Thank you. Goodbye". Sheba's mind started racing, trying to figure out who he was talking to. It was a long ride. Finally they arrived at the hospital. Yes, the local hospital where Hubbie checked her into a psyche ward.

Sheba was checked in and she felt even more hopeless, helpless, and lonely. She felt like a poor prisoner, stripped of all her possessions and dignity. Sheba was not going down like this. All of a sudden she started rebelling. She tried to leave but they stopped her. The doctors and nurses forced her onto the bed and held her down. She struggled mightily saying all kinds of things. All of a sudden she felt a sharp pain and it was over.

The next morning Sheba woke up in a strange bed. She got up and looked around, thinking "Where am I?" She was in a patient's robe and then it hit her. "I am in an insane asylum!" and she felt numb. Slowly she walked out into the hall. There were strangers walking around looking sad. Little did Sheba realize that she looked just like they did. She was hunched over and very frail due to losing twenty three pounds over the last month.

Sheba just knew she was trapped. She thought, "I will probably be here for a long time. Hubbie no longer wants me and my siblings don't love me. I am alive, yet living in hell." The nurse called out, "Sheba Harrington, came here, it is time for your medicine." Sheba thought,"Iit is over, they are going to slowly kill me." She walked over and took the medicine. Daily the hospital had a routine for the patient and Sheba hated it.

Gradually, Sheba started feeling better and thought, "I don't belong here with these crazy people." Hubbie visited her daily and soon her family members and friends started visiting, calling, and bringing nice gifts. Quickly Sheba realized that she was loved and her recovery time was fast. She even started reading the Bible again. Her doctor's witnessed the improvement, but they had to be sure that she was much better since she tried to take her life.

As time went on, Sheba started being that strong woman even in the hospital. She would challenge and question her counselor and doctors. They would listen, take notes, and say "Not yet Sheba". It was a long two weeks. Yes, Sheba was only there for two weeks, but it felt like two years. They released her and then she did outpatient therapy for another three weeks. Guess who returned to work, Sheba!

Three Years Later

Sheba was doing GREAT! Work was going well to the point that top tier clients requested her to work on their projects. She and her sisters were communicating very well. The love between them was much stronger because they realized the importance of family and being there for one another. Sheba started a Brand Management Consulting business. In addition, she even started a non-profit organization focused on: homelessness, domestic violence, educational disparities, youth-at-risk, and international missions. Her first event was a successful golf tournament to raise funds to fight homelessness and domestic violence. Sheba got her groove back plus some!

WITH GOD ALL THINGS ARE POSSIBLE!

Lesson: The human mind is very fragile. If you start feeling stressed and depressed, talk to a family member or close friend and seek professional therapy. Don't be afraid, be proactive!

Lesson: Love God and He will provide all your NEEDS.

Lesson: Love yourself.

Lesson: Knowledge is power and you should develop yourself by obtaining formal and informal training.

Lesson: Obtain multiple degrees and certifications to financially survive in today's society, while planning for the future.

Lesson: Start saving money at an early age and you will secure a bright future.

Lesson: Become independent, always capable of taking care of yourself.

Lesson: Develop and maintain excellent credit.

Lesson: Never look for a husband, let him find you.

Lesson: Work on yourself so when Mr. Right appears, you will be ready.

Lesson: Know that God will NEVER LEAVE YOU NOR FORESAKE YOU!

Lesson: Thank and praise God through the storms, knowing that soon the sun shall shine again.

Lesson: Work hard, play hard, love harder!

Love, Peace, & Blessings,
Sheba

ABOUT THE AUTHOR

REVEREND DR. RITA COLEY

Reverend Dr. Rita Coley is President/CEO of By The Riverside, a faith based organization. An energetic and dynamic presenter she specializes in coaching and retreats for the mind, body and soul. Her seminars and workshops are designed to edify and uplift the inner you. Reverend Coley enjoys the work that encourages others to improve their overall self esteem and communication skills; men, women, teens, couples and parents have benefited personally, socially and professionally. As a former member of the New York County District Attorney's Office, she has had her fair share of numerous personalities, whether it's criminal minds or a co-worker who sat right next to her. Her workshops have revitalized individuals and professionals complaining of "dead-end" relationships and career burnout. She is confident that anyone who leaves her coaching sessions would be revitalized and first rate superb!!

Rita has been a Sunday School Teacher since the age of 13. She employs spiritual disciplines and faith practices in church leadership and her work with youth groups. As both a mentor and advisor Ms. Coley is well respected and sought after in the Tri-State area. Rita is an advisor for a 40 member youth choir with a recent recording who has also had the opportunity to sing for famous recording artists such as Cissy Houston (the late Whitney Houston's mother).

Rita is a member of the NAACP, the Democratic Club Committee and is a former educator for the New York City Board of Education. She is a Certified Life Coach, Professional Diversity Trainer, Youth Trainer, and member of the International Speakers Bureau for the Professional Woman's Network.

God has continuously blessed Rita through her life journey and without God she declares she would be nothing. To God be the Glory for all the things He has done.

Contact:
Company Name: BY THE RIVERSIDE
Address: PO Box 595, Valley Stream, NY 11582
Phone: 516-522-0512
Email: bytheriverside.rc@gmail.com

TEN

Bouncing Back When Grief Strikes

Reverend Dr. Rita Coley

www. Environmentalcaskets.com

Death... what does it mean? When someone passes away, they are no longer breathing has no more brain activity, there is basically no more life. Everyone deals with death in one way or another, whether it's the loss of a loved one or maybe even a pet, whatever the case we all experience some form of death. Some go into deep emotional depression, some choose to go into denial and receive it as nothing happened, some refuse to become sad or upset and celebrate it as a home going meaning entering into heaven. Some people may try to avoid pain altogether. Many become grief stricken for a while and quickly recover and resume normal life activities, people tend to experience several range of emotions, and whether you have experienced one or more of these emotions, death is familiar to everyone, however the most important thing for everyone to know is that in order to heal you must grieve. Grieving is also a coping mechanism. You also must remember that moving forward or continuing with life does not mean that you are forgetting that loved one and many tend to feel guilty in doing so but life for you has to go on.

In 1969, psychiatrist Elisabeth Kübler-Ross introduced what became known as the "five stages of grief," which represent feelings of those who have faced death and tragedy.

1. Denial: "This can't be happening to me."

2. Anger: "Why is this happening? Who is to blame?"

3. Bargaining: "Make this not happen, and in return I will ____."

4. Depression: "I'm too sad to do anything."

5. Acceptance: "I'm at peace with what has happened."

Although these are common responses to loss, there is no structure or timetable for the grieving process.

There will come a time when someone close to us experiences a significant loss. Knowing how to respond to a grieving friend is a good first step in acting as a reliable companion. Many may wonder if they will ever enjoy life again but understanding the process can help you and others to cope and continue on with your life.

Which of these categories do you fall under after you have been given the horrific news that someone you loved has died.

- Feels physically drained

- Can't sleep at night

- Forgetful and unable to think clearly

- Noticeable change in appetite

- Physical distress such as chest pains, headaches or nausea

- Stays extremely busy to avoid thinking about his or her grief

- Eats, drinks watches television, etc. excessively

- Participates in harmful activities

- Senses or dreams about the deceased

- Becomes withdrawn, lonely and apathetic

- Frequent sighing and crying

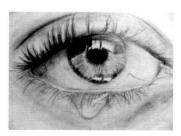

For some death can be experienced in a horrific way, whereas murder or an accident could have occurred, and for some death can be the result of a sickness or long illness that occurred or for some like myself, an all of a sudden death with no warning signs no long illnesses, just a quick overnight passing.

I want to share the experience I had on the night I suddenly lost my younger brother who was only 31 years of age.

He worked for one of the hottest New York radio stations as a DJ. A few days leading up to his death, he had complained to my mother that he had an upset stomach and said to her in a joking manner, "I feel like I am dying". It was dismissed as being something bad he ate. Later I also discovered that he had asked a few of his friends, "What does it mean when you find blood in your urine". That should have been an immediate red flag. It was evident that something was going on wrong in his body. He was not his usual self.

A few days later I was sitting at home one evening after my family had just celebrated my eldest daughter's birthday. The call came close to midnight that he was on his way to my house with his fiancé and he was incoherent and needed to be taken to the emergency room right away. His fiancé was from another borough and did not know how to get there. When they arrived I walked him over to my car and lied him down in the back seat, drove him to the hospital and laid him on the gurney. That would be the last time I would see him alive again. The doctors rushed him into the operating room and I went to register him into the hospital. As I approached the E.R., I opened the door only to see my brother lying on the bed surrounded by doctors who were using a defibrillator to try and revive him. I screamed to the top of my lungs, "WHAT IS HAPPENING TO MY BROTHER" It was a horrible sight. They hurriedly rushed me out of the room. All of his signs of life were shutting down and the doctors were desperately trying to save him. I stood outside the door because I refused to leave his side and I could hear the machines with his heart beat flat line then begin to beat then back to flat line again. It was devastating. I watched the doctors go in and out of his room.... I was pacing the floors and trying to listen in and then..... I heard the heart monitor flat line and I really believed and thought it would start up again but this time it did not. At that point the doctors came out to give me the unbearable news that my brother had just passed away. I couldn't believe it; I was so upset and disappointed. I could remember the doctor asking me "is there anything I can do for you"? and I could remember responding quickly with, could you bring him back to me? With her sad eyes she replied no I'm sorry it's too late, he's gone.

Now the time had come for me to call my parents and get them down to the hospital. This had to be the worst day of my entire life. I remember thinking that I would never want anyone to go through that or trade places with me. My parents arrived at the hospital and I would never forget the look on my mom's face once she was told her baby boy, the youngest of 4 children had just passed away.

After the news had spread the house became a mad house, all through the night people began to come over to pay their respects and offer their condolences and since my brother was a famous D.J. he knew a lot of people who admired and adored him. People starting sharing all of their stories about how he touched their lives and came to their rescue. This was very refreshing to hear about him. This is also a very positive thing to do when someone passes away, it is always refreshing to hear how he positively touched your life and small brief stories that can make you smile. The phone never stopped ringing and the doorbell was constantly being pressed. Many people brought over lots of food and offered up their help.

It was now time for the funeral. My church is fairly large and could hold approximately 350 – 400 people, the church was overfilled. Lines were formed outside that stretched for approximately 3 blocks long of people waiting to get in. I could remember a friend of mine coming up to me at the funeral and saying "OMG Rita, I feel like we are at Elvis Presley's funeral or something" . It was so many people and cars. This showed just how much my brother was loved. My brother had a daughter who at the time was only 7 years old. It was extremely difficult for her as well to lose her father at such a young age. After the initial service which was held in the evening, the next morning was to be the burial. Usually at burials you generally don't have as many people come as they would for the funeral, boy was we wrong. This is not an exaggeration but there were literally approximately 50 plus cars following the Hirsch in the funeral procession. I can remember looking out the limousine's window when we turned a curve and saw and unlimited amount of cars behind us. It was phenomenal. I can remember saying to myself, my brother was adored by the whole world it seemed.

My family got through the funeral and now it was time to try and return to some normalcy. This was extremely hard especially for me, you see, I was the one who took my baby brother to the hospital and he never walked out of there with me again. That is something that is going to lay heavy on my heart for the rest of my life.

I began to withdraw from life. I started thinking am I next? Am I going to die just like my brother died suddenly? I did not want to wear a seat belt in a car because I felt why protect myself I'm going to die anyway! I became very angry and bitter towards life. I did not want to go to any doctor's appointments for check-ups. I basically wanted to give up on life and I could remember saying that I did not like the cards that life had dealt to me.

My kids and my husband began to worry. They would say prayers or grace before a meal and I had refused to join them. I became very angry at God for what had happened. Many didn't believe I had the right to be mad or upset with God but I absolutely did not agree and felt that we were all human and humans become angry when things go ways we don't want them too. God was angry in the bible as well so I felt like who were they to judge me. So I stood my ground and continued to be angry and upset with God. My family was trying everything. Going from a very active member in my church, being on the Usher Board, a Sunday School Teacher, and Advisor for the youth choir, I became very distant and did not want to attend services. What people need to understand is that a person is going to go through grief in their own way. This was my way of battling my grief and many times people do not know what to say to you or how to react around you and your world begins to crumble if you can't come out of it or seek help to regain some normalcy.

My twin daughters were always trying to perk me up or cheer me up, God bless them for trying so hard. I believe God used them to help break me out of my stump because they never gave up on me. They became great conversationalists and they instinctively knew how to make you feel better even if for a moment.

Weeks had passed and I was still mourning. I was simply trying to figure out how I was going to live without my baby brother. I had a lot of soul searching to come to terms with; things I could not control were still haunting at me.

As the days passed on I was still wondering and waiting for this sour feeling I was enduring to dissipate. It was those same lovely twins who finally got me out of my state of funk (as I would call it) and their little prayers and talks that got me to come around finally.

I knew it was a matter of time and I knew it was time to do something about my life because even my marriage was at a standstill. I mean, how do you expect a husband to react to someone who is withdrawn and not as friendly and loving as the person he once met. He tried to help and assist and comfort but I was in my own zone and kept turning him away just like all the others. I could remember my husband saying to other people that he didn't know what to do with me anymore.

Well….. at that very point I knew it was time to snap out of it. No matter how much I mourned or cried or seemed depressed, none of this was ever going to bring my baby brother back. You see, we were and still are a very close knit family. My parents raised us to be close to one another and to always have each other's back. I can still remember the time my late brother and my other siblings would play together as children. We would take family vacations together and my brother and I attended school together from k-12. I was only 18 months older than he. So we were always around each other for most of our life. I can remember when I got my first boyfriend and he became angry with me because I was not spending as much time hanging out with him anymore, so he would automatically dislike my boyfriends. He finally came around when it was time for him to get a girlfriend and understood what it was like to spend your time with your mate. We still did a lot of things together, I even got him a job at my former employer, The New York County District Attorney's Office, he worked on the 2nd floor and I worked on the 7th floor. We would leave for work together and come home together. So you see there was a great closeness there and I finally started to realize why God choose me to be the one to take him to the hospital for him to die in my hands. I now know that God used me to be the strength to try and hold things together, he must have thought I would be the strong one who would be able to endure this tragedy and at first I thought he was crazy and said why me Lord!, then later I began to say WHY NOT ME?

This was a life learning experience and now I can coach people through grief and through a hard loss because I myself have experienced it. I went through a few of the steps mentioned above and I too learned how to cope and continue with life. As I mentioned before, everyone goes through grief differently but it's up to you to find out how to make an individual comfortable as a life coach or even as a close friend or relative, and show that time heals all wounds. After a loved one dies, those who grieve may find it difficult to function in everyday situations. Lingering emotional turmoil, a sense of shock and social withdrawal are painful but natural reactions.

Here are some final thoughts to think about, despite the mentioned expected symptoms, is it possible to become "stuck" in grief? Yes! it is because I became stuck. What if the loss prompts thoughts of self-harm or even suicide? And how can trauma affect the healing process? Symptoms of grief, depression and trauma can resemble one another. In order to respond to these symptoms appropriately and move on with life, it is crucial to understand the differences. Sometimes professional help is needed to determine if you fall into one of these categories.

In conclusion, try and remember that when someone we love is grieving the death of a friend of family member, it's a challenge to know what to do. We all want to try and say the right things to the person, you should also always show support which helps in the healing process and shows them they are not alone in this.

At times we may end up awkwardly offering advice, sputtering something spiritual or avoiding the situation altogether, one thing to remember to say when all else is confusing is simply," 'I'm so sorry for your loss.' ", also you can:

Be there to listen. "It's always tempting to give advice, but don't. True empathy, encouragement and compassion will help those going through a difficult time.

State specifically how you're able to help. Offer to prepare a meal, provide a ride, or help clean and sort through old items. Be sensitive to your friends or family member's feelings and be proactive when it comes to meeting needs,

Remind your loved one to take time out to rest, and to hold off on any major life decisions. It is undoubtedly draining to adjust to a loss and this impairs the ability to think clearly as well as make any final decisions and lastly,

Reach out when your friend most misses a loved one. Often time's people seem to disappear or slow down on calls once the funeral and arrangements are completed, and a lot of times people still need you around them, they don't want you to disappear when all is over and all too often this happens. "Holidays and anniversaries will often trigger the grief response, even many years later. "Those are good times to be extra supportive and loving."

Among those mourning a death, some find the pain diminishes within weeks, months or maybe even years. It is best to arrive at a place of acceptance, peace and hope for the future. You should always reminisce about your deceased loved one instead of feeling consumed by memories.

I am Rita Coley and I am the President of By the Riverside, Life Coaching. If you would like to contact me, please reach out to me at 516-522-0512.

You won't forget but you will be able to move on in life!

ABOUT THE AUTHOR

JODI BROCKINGTON

Jodi Brockington, is a Senior Executive with more than 15 years of experience in myriad roles including prospecting and cultivating high profile clients, stakeholders and networks, managing daily operations, events, conferences and programs.

Some of her most recent work includes serving as Deputy Director for Speaker Management for the Global Financial Dignity Summit and Chief Marketing Officer for Count Me in for Women's Economic Independence. A well-sought after speaker, Jodi has been featured as a Presenter at the 2013 Black Enterprise Women of Power Summit, where she was invited back to present a crash course on how to connect effectively and with confidence at the 2014 Summit. She has also served as a speaker for the New York State Bar Association Women's Group on social media, apps for career success and ethics. In addition, she was a speaker at Baruch School of Public Affairs on How to Use Linkedin for Networking Your Way to Career Success.

Her award honors include NIARA Consulting being recognized as the 2013 Best Overall Business Award from Stiletto Woman Media, the 2012 Beauty & Beat Heroines of Excellence Award, a NV Magazine 2011 Mover and Shaker Award, The Network Journal "40 Under 40" Award and an Urban Influencer Award from the National Urban League.

Jodi has been featured in print publications and digital media such as TrendSetters Magazine, Racing Towards Diversity Magazine, NV Magazine, The BOSS Network, and NV.com. She has also been featured in two books, "CRAVE New York" and "Leading from the Middle—Conversations with Successful Middle Managers, and had the pleasure of hosting the National Urban League's Small Business Matters Pitch Contest in Philadelphia.

Jodi earned Master's degrees from the University of Southern California in Social Work; from Baruch College in Public Affairs; and from the Hunter College School of Education. She completed her undergraduate studies at UCLA.

ELEVEN

Time Waits for No One

Jodi Brockington

What does breast cancer, a car accident and surgery all have in common? For most people not much, but for me they were opportunities for me to learn more about just how powerful tragic life experiences and myself can be. These three unrelated things provided hope and lessons for me to learn from that have not only allowed me to survive, but to thrive and help others do the same. Throughout my life, there have been so many people who have shown me that even through pain, sickness and tragedy in our lives, it is possible to find value, meaning and purpose out of major life crises.

Never underestimate the power of a seatbelt or a cell phone; both of these things saved my life many years ago allowing me to write about it today. You never know when you get in car and hit the road or simply leave your house what is going to happen to you-but you never (at least not me) think that there is going to be something bad-but you never know.

In my case, I had been going on an annual house boat trip on Lake Mead (past Las Vegas and Laughlin) for many years with some of my true Los Angeles born and bred friends that I had made over the years of being in school at UCLA and USC. Every Memorial Day weekend we would ALL pile into cars, trucks, and minivans and hit the road at the end of the day. The group had been expanding each year either by marriage, new friends, kids, etc. and I extended an invitation to another New Yorker to join the LA crew for this trip. He was new to LA, not really "feeling the LA scene" and thought this would help him get better connected and create some new friends since he was going to be in LA for a while for business.

Long story short, for the trip everyone was responsible for bringing different things food, extra gas for the jet-skis, etc. This year we were responsible for the alcohol for the entire group for the entire weekend for about 25-30 people. Let's just say our small truck was filled to the brim with alcohol and our things. It had been a long day for everyone-we had all been either working all day, in school or whatever. We had been on the road for at least a few hours and I could tell that the driver was getting tired-kind of nodding and talking less as we continued to drive.

When we stopped at the designated rest stop with everyone- I asked if he wanted me to drive (which I HATE to do-but could really tell he needed some rest) and he took me up on the offer. He slept for the next couple of hours while I drove and we made it to the last big grocery store for any final food supplies and anything else anyone might have forgotten It was the final stop before we get to the Lake to unload everything and get on our designated houseboats for the weekend. Needless to say, the driver and I never made it to the lake that weekend. Instead, I almost ended up dead if it wasn't that I had my seatbelt on, was slightly reclined in my seat and that we turned over 4 times to the inside of the cliff instead of the outside. I was knocked unconscious from the sunroof and the impact of the truck turning over 4 times and probably shock. All I remember was telling the driver to wake up, the car skidding from side to side, the smell of alcohol. The next thing I knew, I was in pain, asking for my Mom thinking I was in an ambulance, but really was being helicoptered to UNLV Hospital.

When we got to the hospital I had my clothes cut open, because they had to revive me, glass embedded everywhere from head to toe, my back, neck and knees were killing me and there were people everywhere. All I could remember was the skidding. In addition to my seatbelt and angle of my seat, it was the driver's cellphone that truly saved me because emergency 911 could be called to come and get us. The only identification I had on me at the time was my California driver's license and my Mother's business card in Paris.

They contacted my Mom, who contacted my Dad who contacted my roommate and close friend Audrey. Audrey and her brother Julian drove ALL the way from LA to get me and then officially became family. I was a still in a lot of pain-but my HMO medical insurance at the time would only allow for a few day stay and since my Mom was flying to Los Angeles the next day from Paris. I was a mess-I had a neck brace, a knee brace, cuts everywhere from all the glass that had shattered onto and into my body as well as crutches. Let's just say it was a LONG ride home. Nobody was comfortable and the drive took forever since it was the holiday weekend.

It was like being a child again. I could not do much of anything so my Mother was doing it all from cleaning, bathing, washing my hair, etc. I was on medical leave from work since I could not walk or drive to work-this was a blessing a curse at the same time. As much as I did not like my current job and really hated being at home with nothing to do either. So, I found a volunteer opportunity to help fundraising for an organization called "Real Men Cook" that needed someone to follow up with sponsors, out reach to male volunteers to cook for the event and all of the logistical partners-vendors, venue, etc.

My Father came out a couple of weeks after my Mom left to see me with his own two eyes. By the time he came to Los Angeles to visit and continue my care I was feeling a lot better able to move around on my crutches, still had the neck brace and my leg wrapped in an ace bandage. My Dad was helpful since he could drive me around (and my mother could not). He took me to the DMV to get my third red handicapped placard, which was a grueling task because you had to actually go to the DMV, get on a LONG line, get a new one and pay for it. Which then got me to ask my doctor at my next visit if he was just stalling-not telling me that my back injury and knees were not going to get better. He said that I was always going to have back issues and was uncertain about my knees at this time-let's just say, I got a blue handicapped placard at my next and last visit to the DMV.

I had decided that I really wanted to make a career move and leave my current workplace. It was not a healthy work environment and I was being overworked and underpaid. Against my Father's judgment, he drove me to a few job interviews with other leading nonprofit organizations where I knew the founders or those in leadership roles to at least do informational interviews.

I did not get a new job right away, I went back to my same workplace but with a new role that they gave me since I was out on disability leave they had to give me a position with the organization, but it did not have to be the same position. This just propelled me to get out of there sooner and I did. I grew a lot closer to Audrey, my roommate and co-worker she is more of the big sister I always wanted – we are still just as close today and continue to help each other through the ups and downs in our lives. I was NOT going to let crutches and some other physical injuries stop me from going after my goals.

What being on disability at the age of 24 taught me is that anything can happen to anyone at anytime. There are systems in place to help you some that you can control better than others like family and friends and others you cannot-like medical insurance policies and HR policies. Always take time to evaluate and listen to your instincts about things personally and professionally. I need to learn to ask for help more, realize that it is okay to not be able to do everything-at least not all at one time and that people do want to help me. Lastly, the fact that I survived this tragic accident, there was still more for me to do and that time waits for no one… this is why I am committed to motivating others and try to find the silver lining in every cloud.

*****

I must point out, that it was/is not me who had breast cancer, it was my best friend Allison Fisher, who provided me the opportunity to learn more about the disease than I ever imagined, medical systems around the world, alternative medicine and mostly about living!!!

The old saying is still true: It's not what happens to you, it's how you handle what happens to you that counts. In the case with Allison, I thought since she had already beat the odds once and her cancer went into remission it was never going to come back. So, after her first fight with cancer and winning the battle, Allison decided to go back to school to get her MBA at UCLA. However, it returned…not right away, but in her last quarter since UCLA is a quarter system.

I must say that it was the entire journey with Allison, her family and other close friends that truly taught me lessons that I use everyday. I never thought of myself as one of those cure seekers-staying up late, going through library files, asking everyone I knew who had a friend or family member with breast cancer what they were doing or had done. Every moment I had to spend on finding a solution for Allison's cancer I did. We were ALL on TEAM ALLISON without even recognizing how it impacted our own lives. She tried everything from traditional medicine, chemotherapy to alternative medicine and potions.

We did everything in our power to make ALL of Allison's dreams come true hoping she had ALL the time in the world to make them happen and also NOT knowing how much time she had left to live. These were the places I lived in my mind and in my life daily-often losing sleep and not knowing why-mostly because I was afraid that I would miss something or that it would be Allison's last moment alive.

We went to amusement parks, ate all kinds of really bad (but extremely good) foods that she loved, wanted to try and/or simply wanted to have from some of her favorite places. There was not a place that she wanted to go to or eat at that someone did not take her to. The most memorable time I had was traveling to Hawaii with Allison and our 3rd Musketeer Karen. It was this trip that truly defined just how important friendship is and why I give it so much value. Allison was that person who not only did we share our astrological sign, but who if I ever got married or had children was to be my maid of honor and Godmother to my children, etc. We also learned the value of travel to just be FREE from everyone and everything for a moment-no medication, no parents, no boyfriends, no work, no schedule-no RULES!!! However, being thankful to have ALL of those things.

I even went to church with Allison-not an unfamiliar place for me to go, but it was NOT my every Sunday destination-but it was for Allison. I really got to learn more about her and my spiritual side during this time…Faithful Central became a place for both of us to say nothing to each other and breathe for a moment and simply listen, look through the referred to passages in the Bible and take away lessons to talk about over brunch.

I regret that Allison was NOT a survivor in her second battle with cancer, but the rest of us she left behind were able to survive and thrive. You never really know the power of a person until you meet their family-by this I mean ALL of their family, friends, classmates, colleagues and those who simply just know you from the volunteer work you did. That was Allison.

I had mixed feelings about going to Baltimore for her funeral-I was still shocked that she had not won the battle that she had won before-Allison was a true fighter. I had never been to a funeral before and this was going to be the first one and it was for my best friend-not a criminal, who someone caught by a stray bullet in a shooting, or from a bad situation. Allison was one of those people who everyone loved and wanted to know, that those like me who were fortunate enough to have in our lives will never forget.

I could not walk to the casket for the viewing-too much for me to take in all at once and I wanted to remember her as I always knew here and that person was gone. Plenty of others paid their final respect and took their final look of Allison while I sat in the back of the church watching and wishing this was just a bad dream. I knew it was not a dream when one of her close classmates recited a poem "Angel with a Jazz Note" which described Allison perfectly where even the poet was moved and not a dry eye in the church.

With Allison's spirit, family and other close friends we started a nonprofit in her name The Allison Fisher Fund. To raise money to help other students at American University and UCLA have the same opportunities as Allison did to go to college and graduate school.

What my Angel taught me is that life is short, you must go after your dreams and do not let others stop you find those who will support you and make sure they too dream BIG. She also let me see just how family and friends are your true strength, are always there with you, even when you do not see them all the time-it is their love and help that you depend on because it is ALWAYS. Lastly, that although like her, others may come and go from my life that I can always keep what I need from them with me-those memories and feelings are forever.

*****

Who knew that a workout fanatic, working at a healthy beverage company, testing every bootcamp, cleanse, gluten free recipes, vegetarian food only, vegan dessert eating person like myself would end up having major surgery in three months time??? Not me and not anyone else who knew me. My usual routine a few years ago was going to the gym everyday or at least taking some kind of fitness class from Bootcamp, Soul Cycle, Yoga, TRX, etc. I was definitely in shape, but who couldn't be in better shape-so I always pushed myself to do more.

The night before I was heading out of town for a Leadership Development Fellowship I was not feeling well. My stomach was bloated-which I almost never experience, a lot of pressure on my side and I was unable to get comfortable sitting down, laying down standing up, etc. I had a very upset stomach and felt like I needed to throw up...I did but nothing much came up and I did NOT feel any better and ended up in the emergency room.

That night I was told that I had food poisoning-they gave me a mint Maalox mix and fluids through me-while this was going on-against his will my Father went to get my packed bag for my trip. My Dad returned by the time the fluids were done and we went to pay and check out of the hospital. I was feeling a LOT better, but NOT 100% but caught a cab to the airport and my Dad took another one home.

I survived the flight and the entire first meeting of my Leadership Development Fellowship. I had to stick to a BRAT diet while I was there –bread, rice, apples and toast-all I remember was bland and wanting to eat what everyone else was having. I was glad to be there, still not feeling well, but knowing that I would have missed a LOT had I not been there. Traveling home we had a layover and my stomach started feeling bad again, so I bought TUMS to try to get rid of the gas. They helped some but not completely.

The next day I went to see my own doctor-who then sent me a few blocks away for some x-rays. Even laying on the x-ray table was uncomfortable and when the technician said she wanted to speak with the doctor and have him come in and look, I knew that was not a good sign. What was annoying was that they are not allowed to tell you anything-so luckily my doctor's office was only a few blocks away, but walking those few blocks felt like a marathon. My doctor told me that I had an infected gall bladder and that I would have to be on major antibiotics to get rid of the infection. I followed the doctor's orders and felt much better. However, a couple of weeks later a good friend was in town so we went to dinner at my favorite Ethiopian food. On the way home I started getting that same uneasy and gas feeling I had come to know as well as feeling sweaty. I decided to take a shower and in the shower started throwing up-so I called my doctor, got dressed and was told to go to the hospital to meet up with a specialist Dr. Marc

Greenberg. I ended up throwing up in the emergency admittance area and then in the hospital for nearly two weeks until they figured out what was wrong with me. Everyday was my own episode of Greys Anatomy with early morning visits from a team of diverse medical interns eager to find out what was wrong with me. Daily visits from old and new friends, and my Dad was there everyday for the entire visiting hours and making sure that anyone who came to visit me felt like part of the family.

When I checked out I was told that I had to get rid of all of the infection before they could operate and it would take about a month. I would need to be on a strict diet of nothing but fruits and vegetables, water, tea and the antibiotics I was given. I followed Dr. Greenberg's orders and had my gall bladder removed on December 23rd and asked for my holiday gift to be home for Christmas and I was. There were a few complications and I did not leave the hospital that same day as originally planned I stayed overnight and was released into my Father's care on Christmas Eve day.

The healing took quite some time and during this time of trying to get better and deal with my physical pain, the startup company I was working for let me go, I was owed money by someone who did not pay a sublease of my apartment in Harlem and really did not know what would be next for me. However, I could not focus on all my challenges, I needed to concentrate on getting better.

While being bed bound I had a LOT of time to think. I decided that I wanted to go back to working for myself after trying to help others with their startup. It took months for me to get back on my feet and very few people were aware of my health condition and I did not want people to know thought it might not be good for my career. I had some money saved, was able to get on unemployment, continued to remain active on social media and look for my next clients. In a few months with the support of my family and friends, I was able to get back on my feet and continue my career success ladder as if nothing happened.

What I learned from this experience is that you cannot do anything without your health and without the help of others. You need to do the things that really are important and true to who you are, and not what others believe is right for you. If you are unable to move, have the energy to get through a day to even think you are just as good as being dead. Without your health are unable to do anything for yourself or help anyone else. I have made health the main focus of my life and my work and a try to inspire others to make it a priority in theirs. I have incorporated this into my brand and I am now a certified indoor cycling and fitness instructor.

We live in challenging times, when even the most successful among us may occasionally become overwhelmed by problems relating to money, marriage, parenting, illness, stress, or any of the myriad challenges we all face from time to time.

What do these comebacks prove? That no matter what your problem or background, where you're from or the mistakes you've made, it's possible to stage a comeback, even when things seem hopeless. Half the battle is realizing that whatever YOU want to do can be done; the other half is the specific strategy you need to implement to make it happen-and NEVER do it ALONE.

ABOUT THE AUTHOR

MARKHETA PARKER

Markheta Parker is a published Author. She is also the founder of Parker Notary Mobile Services, a business focused on helping businesses and customers. She is helping businesses and customers reduce liability risk and prevention of fraud. She authenticates loan and legal document signings. She has a telecommunication background with over twenty-five years' experience in the business. She is working at a Fortune 500 telecommunication company.

Education: Bachelor's degree in Liberal Studies from Roosevelt University, and a Certificate in Marketing Strategy from Cornell University.

Markheta is also a member of The Professional Woman Network, Non Fiction Authors Association, and National Association of Professional Women.

Contact:
Markheta Parker
P.O. Box 314
Independence MO 64051
Telephone: 816-392-9887
Email: markhetap@aol.com
Website: http://about.me/markhetaparker

TWELVE

Overcoming Fear in an Uncertain World

Markheta Parker

A re there any solutions to overcoming fear? Could it be that uncertainty in the world produces fear in us? I realized learning to overcome fear is about facing my fears with courage. Problem solving principles will set us on the path to overcoming fear, change our uncertain world into a life of courage, provide hope, and personal growth.

To begin, twenty-one years ago, I stood shaking in a state of fear. I stood in my second floor apartment overlooking Hyde Park in Chicago. Fear quickly seized me, as I realized my life choice decision had just been decided. I could feel my body lean in the direction of the green couch in the living room; however my paralyzing feeling of uncertainty would not allow me to move. Oh, how I wanted to sit down and think. I eventually realize my fear was just a symptom of the unknown. The unknown creates that paralyzing feeling that causes us to be uncertain. The environment in which we live, our daily interaction with people and all of life experiences is constantly changing. We can make a conscious effort, to stay focus, as we look for solutions to overcome our fears.

We gain strength, and courage, and confidence by each experience in which we really stop to look fear in the face... we must do that which we think we cannot. —Eleanor Roosevelt

At the same time, you see, I had just entered a rental agreement on a townhouse with a coworker through a relocation agent. The townhouse was in another state. I had never seen the townhouse, much less been to the state of Missouri. Why did I make this decision? My life choice decision was a result of an office closing and relocating to another position within the same corporation. Sometimes we have to make uncomfortable choices simple because it is best for us, family, and friends. We feel a shock of fear and uncertainty, because we are leaving that area of comfort. We can move from this area of comfort successfully, through courage.

The ache for home lives in all of us, the safe place where we can go as we are and not be questioned. —Maya Angelou

First of all, I knew deep within me, this would change my relationship with my family and friends. This breaking news would have an impact on my family and friends. This paralyzing feeling of fear began to live my body, tears filled my eyes and the feeling of sadness hit me. We were in the middle of the school year in Chicago. My son was in kindergarten. I knew this life choice decision would change the entire direction of my life forever. I knew, at that moment courage and hope was part of the solution.

After that, I walked slowing toward the picture window in my living room looking out. I stood there taking in the view of the landscape of Hyde Park. Tall beautiful green trees lined each side of the sidewalks. I studied the tree leafs, as the gentle wind passed around the trees. I watched, as each individual green leaf seemed to dance in the gentle wind. Each branch served as platform for the green leafs. The green leafs moved back and forth in the gentle wind. My eyes glanced at the concrete side walk and back into the greenery in the courtyard. My eyes took in the beauty of each flower. I snapped out of glance, because of the loud thump a car made hitting a bump coming down the street. I had a strong sense of motivation at that moment. I realized this was a great opportunity for personal growth.

> *In all things of nature there is something of the marvelous.*
> —Aristotle

In addition, I established my problem solving principles plan. This plan is for goal setting, brainstorming ideas and serves as a plan of action. You see, I had two weeks to relocate successfully out of state. At this point, I was focused, motivated and determined to be a success without obstacles in my way. This is a workable plan and it got me the results I needed.

If I show you my problem solving techniques, would you be interested?

Yes? _____

Get you pen ready to take notes and answer questions. Are you ready to get started? Is that ok? _____

Yes? _____

Problem Solving Principles Plan

Name: _____

First, Inspirational Quotes set the mood to be inspired, motivated, and encouraged. Write down 3 Inspirational Quotes. The topics can be about overcoming fear, courage, fear, hope, and personal growth, life choices and self-improvement.

1. Quote

_____

_____

_____

2. Quote

_____

_____

_____

3. Quote

_____

_____

_____

Second, Music will set the mood to be inspired, motivated, and encouraged. Write down 3 CDs. Make a commitment to listen exclusively to your 3 choices. Write down the name of each CD including the artist's name.

1. Music CD

_____

_____

2. Music CD

_____

_____

3. Music CD

_____

_____

Third, what is my strategy in developing friendships with those that inspire me to be my best?

1. _____

_____

_____

Fourth, what is my strategy for avoiding toxic friendships?

1. _____

_____

_____

Next, write down the meaning of each word below. How will each word meaning be applied as a problem solving technique when issues arise? See list of fourteen problem solving techniques below.

1. Overcoming fear _____

_____

2. Uncertain_____

_____

3. Courage_____

_____

4. Hope _____

_____

5. Personal Growth _____

_____

6. Life Choices_____

_____

7. Motivation_____

_____

8. Stress _____

_____

9. Self-help_____

_____

10. Self-improvement _____

_____

11. Resources_____

_____

12. Solution_____

_____

13. Technique _____

_____

14. Principles _____

_____

In addition, write your personal statement of commitment.

_____

_____

_____

_____

_____

_____

_____

_____

An equally important, fact is you have just travel the path in overcoming your fears in this uncertain world. The path you took is through the Problem Solving Principles Plan. During your travel on this path, you went through personal growth. We studied how to apply all 14 problem solving techniques. We have established that problem solving principles will set us on the path to overcoming fear, change our uncertain world into a life of courage, provide hope, and personal growth. I am living proof this works.

Notes:

_____

_____

_____

_____

_____

_____

_____

_____

_____

_____

_____

_____

_____

_____

_____

_____

_____

_____

_____

_____

_____

ABOUT THE AUTHOR

STACY L. HENDERSON, PhD

Stacy L. Henderson, PhD, is the Founder and President of Dr. Stacy L. Henderson & Associates, a firm which specializes in personal and professional development through coaching, consulting and training. She conducts seminars and workshops that have been presented nationwide and abroad. Her training topics include: Self-Esteem and Empowerment, Women as Leaders, Enhancing Your Professional Image, Dealing with Change & Transition and Teen Etiquette to name a few. Dr. Henderson has been trained and certified by the Professional Woman Network (PWN). She is a Certified Professional Coach, Certified Youth Trainer and is internationally recognized a Certified Diversity Trainer, specializing in Women's Issues. She is a contributing author for the following books in the PWN African-American Library: Wellness for the African-American Woman: Mind, Body and Spirit; Raising African-American Boys; Raising African-American Girls; and The Woman's Handbook for Self-Confidence - which are available nationally and in the Caribbean.

Dr. Henderson has a Bachelor of Science in Education, with a Specialization in Workforce Education and Development; a Master of Arts in Health Services Management; and Doctorates in Business Administration and Christian Leadership. She is a member of the Professional Woman Network (PWN), the National Association of Female Executives (NAFE), the American College of Health Care Executives (ACHE), Delta Sigma Theta Sorority, Inc., and National Naval Officers' Association.

Dr. Henderson is dedicated to motivating individuals to achieve their best mental, physical and spiritual health. She is available to consult on a local, national and international basis. She is available for individual and group coaching and consulting sessions, religious functions, military events, youth assemblies, seminars and conferences.

Contact:
Dr. Stacy L. Henderson & Associates
Personal & Professional Coaching and Consulting
P. O. Box 886913
Great Lakes, Illinois 60088-6913
Email: SLHenderson007@aol.com
www.protrain.net

THIRTEEN

Stepping Out on Faith

Dr. Stacy L. Henderson

"Now faith is the substance of things hoped for, the evidence of things not seen."—Hebrews 11:1

Introduction

Faith is not only believing in, but being confident of the things that God promises. We must go before Him, believing all things. How do we acquire faith? *"So then faith cometh by hearing, and hearing by the word of God."*— (Romans 10:17). Thus, finding out what the Bible says about faith is very important. Faith can be defined in a number of different ways.

However, if we want to know how God defines faith, the Bible must be used as the reference source. Furthermore, God's definition of faith supersedes any and all other definitions derived by man.

It is helpful to remember that there are all kinds of faith in the world. And we all believe in different manners and exhibit our faith in a myriad of ways. Faith is an integral component of our belief system for a number of reasons. For example:

1. **Faith is necessary to please God** – *"But without faith it is impossible to please him: for he that cometh to God must believe that he is, and that he is a rewarder of them that diligently seek him."* —Hebrews 11:6.

2. **Faith is essential for our salvation** – *"For it is by grace you have been saved, through faith—and this not from yourselves, it is the gift of God."*—Ephesians 2:8.

3. **Faith is vital for self-preservation: if we do not want God to destroy us or to die in our sins, we must believe** – *"I said therefore unto you, that ye shall die in your sins: for if ye believe not that I am He, ye shall die in your sins."*—John 8:24.

4. **There are many people who do not have faith** – *"But there are some of you that believe not. For Jesus knew from the beginning who they were that believed not, and who should betray him."* —John 6:64.

5. **Evil forces believe in the true and living God** – *"Thou believest that there is one God; thou doest well: the devils also believe, and tremble."*— James 2:19.

   Note: Now, I ask you: "If the evil forces believe in God, why don't you?"

Laying a Firm Foundation for Our Faith

Usually when we speak about faith we instantly think of Thomas. He is often referred to as 'Doubting Thomas' because of his statement, *"Except I shall see in his hands the print of the nails, and put my finger into the print of the nails, and thrust my hand into his side, I will not believe."* (John 20:25). After Thomas personally saw Jesus appear in a room where he was gathered with the other disciples, and he was able to feel – with his own hands – the holes that were pierced in Jesus' hands and side, only then did he believe. Jesus replied, *"Because thou hast seen me, thou hast believed: Blessed are they that have not seen, and yet have believed."* (John 20:29).

Although none of us have seen Christ literally, the evidence of his existence is everywhere.

The simple fact that you and I exist is proof of our Creator. *"And to make all men see what is the fellowship of the mystery, which from the beginning of the world hath been hid in God, who created all things by Jesus Christ."* (Ephesians 3:9)

God only reveals to us a little at a time. If we are faithful, He will show more of His will to us.

The more we align ourselves to God's will, the more we will experience Him. That is why we must have a relationship with Him and ensure that we endeavor to strengthen that bond as we go through our daily walk along life's journey. When we have a strong bond with God, we are better able to handle the trials and tribulations that we will experience in life. One principle the Bible shows is that God will test our faithfulness before He increases us. One such example is illustrated in Matthew 25:14-30:

¹⁴ *For the kingdom of heaven is as a man travelling into a far country, who called his own servants, and delivered unto them his goods.*

¹⁵ *And unto one he gave five talents, to another two, and to another one; to every man according to his several ability; and straightway took his journey.*

¹⁶ *Then he that had received the five talents went and traded with the same, and made them other five talents.*

¹⁷ *And likewise he that had received two, he also gained other two.*

¹⁸ *But he that had received one went and digged in the earth, and hid his lord's money.*

¹⁹ *After a long time the lord of those servants cometh, and reckoneth with them.*

²⁰ *And so he that had received five talents came and brought other five talents, saying, Lord, thou deliveredst unto me five talents: behold, I have gained beside them five talents more.*

²¹ *His lord said unto him, Well done, thou good and faithful servant: thou hast been faithful over a few things, I will make thee ruler over many things: enter thou into the joy of thy lord.*

²² *He also that had received two talents came and said, Lord, thou deliveredst unto me two talents: behold, I have gained two other talents beside them.*

²³ *His lord said unto him, Well done, good and faithful servant; thou hast been faithful over a few things, I will make thee ruler over many things: enter thou into the joy of thy lord.*

24 *Then he which had received the one talent came and said, Lord, I knew thee that thou art an hard man, reaping where thou hast not sown, and gathering where thou hast not strawed:*

25 *And I was afraid, and went and hid thy talent in the earth: lo, there thou hast that is thine.*

26 *His lord answered and said unto him, Thou wicked and slothful servant, thou knewest that I reap where I sowed not, and gather where I have not strawed:*

27 *Thou oughtest therefore to have put my money to the exchangers, and then at my coming I should have received mine own with usury.*

28 *Take therefore the talent from him, and give it unto him which hath ten talents.*

29 *For unto every one that hath shall be given, and he shall have abundance: but from him that hath not shall be taken away even that which he hath.*

30 *And cast ye the unprofitable servant into outer darkness: there shall be weeping and gnashing of teeth.*

This passage, I believe, aims to teach us that God knows what our abilities are. And He tests us based on those abilities in order to prove who is faithful and who is not. Talent refers to a considerable sum of money in this particular passage. The first two servants were faithful with what they were given. They were focused on the Lord rather than themselves. They did not seek riches or wealth – they sought the Kingdom.

The lazy servant, on the other hand, was quite the opposite. He was self-centered and greedy. He was more concerned about the cost he might have to pay than the sacrifice itself. He did not have the kind of love for the Lord that made him desire to work for the Lord's benefit.

God knows our hearts and He knows us best. When we begin our Christian walk, we are just babes in Christ. Thus, at that point we are oftentimes focused on ourselves. Unfortunately, many remain self-centered simply because we do not want to pay the cost of sacrifice. Until we abandon the notion of fulfilling our own desires, we will never see anything but fear of missing out on our lives. In Luke 9:23-24, Jesus says, *"If anyone desires to come after Me, let him deny himself, and take up his cross daily, and follow Me. For whoever desires to save his life will lose it, but whoever loses his life for My sake will save it."*

Do you believe that? Where is your faith?

Faith is an Action Word

Do you believe in the promises of God? He keeps His promises. You have to seek the kingdom of God first. Many promises have something that is necessary for us to do in order for us to claim them. However, God does not ask much from us. He simply wants us to believe in Him, trust Him, listen to Him or just love Him. Do you want the promises of God fulfilled for you? Do you believe in the Promise Keeper?

Here are a few of God's promises. Of course, those listed require action on our part:

"Fear thou not; for I am with thee: be not dismayed; for I am thy God: I will strengthen thee; yea, I will help thee; yea, I will uphold thee with the right hand of my righteousness."—Is 41:10

"But let him ask in faith, nothing wavering. For he that wavereth is like a wave of the sea driven with the wind and tossed."—James 1:6

"If ye abide in me, and my words abide in you, ye shall ask what ye will, and it shall be done unto you."—John 15:7

"... He that believeth on me, the works that I do shall he do also; and greater works than these shall he do; because I go unto my Father. And whatsoever ye shall ask in my name, that will I do, that the Father may be glorified in the Son. If ye shall ask any thing in my name, I will do it."
—John 14:12-14

If you believe in God and have faith in His Word, then God wants you to act on your faith. Here are a few verses that call us to put our faith in action:

1. 1 Timothy 6:11 – *"pursue ... faith"*

2. 1 Timothy 6:11 – *"Fight the good fight of the faith."*

3. 1 Peter 5:9 – *"Resist him (the devil), standing firm in the faith."*

4. 1 Timothy 4:12 – *"Be thou an example for the believers in speech, in life, in love, in faith and in set and purity."*

5. 2 Corinthians 13:5 – *"Examine yourselves to see whether you are in the faith; test yourselves."*

6. 2 Corinthians 8:7 – *"Excel in everything—in faith, in speech, in knowledge, in complete earnestness."*

7. 2 Peter 1:5 – *"Make every effort to add to your faith goodness; and to goodness, knowledge."*

8. 2 Timothy 2:22 – *"Flee the evil desires of youth, and pursue righteousness, faith, love and peace."*

9. Ephesians 6:16 – *"Take up the shield of faith, with which you can extinguish all the flaming arrows of the evil one."*

10. Psalm 46:10 – *"Be still, and know that I am God."* (Even when we are commanded to wait on the Lord, it requires that we exercise our faith).

Stepping Out

It is crucial to understand that in order for God's promises to be kept for us, we must obey and follow Him. There is one important thing that we have to do in order to claim any of God's promises: we have to believe that the promise is true. Oftentimes we find it difficult to believe something we can not see, but that is where faith enters in. We must believe that God's Word is true; then we have to claim the promises of God. He tells us in His Word that 'faith without works is dead.'

God increases our faith by rescuing and delivering us from our troubles. He strengthens us by making us strong in Him. He also tries to teach us to look to Him as our deliverer. God has proven Himself time and time again through miracles and wonders – some of which we do not see until we take a moment of solitude and reflect over our lives.

But a time will come when God will ask you to prove your faith. Keep in mind that faith is belief (and trust) in action. Simply believing in God is not enough. Faith is putting our total trust in the Lord – even when the odds are against us. It is during those times when it appears all hope is gone, God is simply teaching us that He sustains us and that we are not sufficient in ourselves.

The Bible is filled with stories (paraphrased) of the faithful:

1. ***David***, *who, when just a young shepherd boy, faced Goliath - a giant and a man of war. When he faced Goliath, he did not give defeat a second thought. He had complete confidence that God would be with him.* —1 Samuel 17

2. ***Abraham*** *had such strong faith in God that he was willing to sacrifice his only son at God's request.* —Hebrews 11:17

3. *By faith the walls of **Jericho** fell, after the people had marched around them for seven days.* —Hebrews 11:30

4. *By faith he made his home in the promised land like a stranger in a foreign country; he lived in tents, as did **Isaac and Jacob**, who were heirs with him of the same promise.* —Hebrews 11:9

5. *By faith **Noah**, when warned about things not yet seen, built an ark to save his family. By his faith he condemned the world and became heir of the righteousness that comes by faith.* —Hebrews 11:7

6. *By faith **Jacob**, when he was dying, blessed each of Joseph's sons, and worshiped as he leaned on the top of his staff.* —Hebrews 11:21

7. *Some men brought to him a paralytic, lying on a mat. When **Jesus** saw their faith, he said to the paralytic, "Take heart, son; your sins are forgiven."* —Matthew 9:2

8. *By faith Isaac blessed **Jacob and Esau** in regard to their future.* —Hebrews 11:20

9. *By faith* **Abraham***, even though he was past age—and Sarah herself was barren—was enabled to become a father because he considered him faithful who had made the promise.* —Hebrews 11:11

Conclusion

When we are willing to step out in faith, even when we do not think we will be successful, God's power enables us to succeed. I believe this is the only way to be exalted by God. Our response to His call to action empowers us with a deeper form of faith. When we are stretched beyond ourrealm of imagination and what we *think* are impossibilities, that is actually God at work in us through our faith in Him.

In summary, faith is something that God requires of us. It is the first in a true, meaningful relationship with Him. By having faith in God, it increases our love for him. As our love for God grows, so does our commitment to Him. Our faith in God and our love of God go hand-in-hand. Our faith can be measured by the amount of courage that we have. Our commitment to God and our trust in His power determines our level of faith in Him.

And, according to His Word, our faith only needs to be the size of a mustard seed – *"Because of your little faith. For truly, I say to you, if you have faith like a grain of mustard seed, you will say to this mountain, 'Move from here to there,' and it will move, and nothing will be impossible for you."*—Matthew 17:20.

Note: All scripture references were taken from the King James Version of the Holy Bible.

Notes:

ABOUT THE AUTHOR

WANDA H. PEMBERTON

Wanda H. Pemberton, Founder and CEO of Sirrah Image Consulting, has a passion for helping others put their best foot forward in business and in life. Sirrah Image Consulting was created to help others align, refine, and re-define the way they present themselves to the world. The goal is to help clients become more polished, strategic and intentional, while maintaining their authenticity.

After graduating from the University of North Carolina, at Chapel Hill in 1986, with a BA in Sociology, Wanda continued to embrace her love of learning. In 2006, she received an MBA (with an emphasis in organizational psychology and development) and a certificate in Human Resource Management. Wanda has been employed with the federal government for over 25 years and is currently pursuing a PhD in Psychology, through Walden University.

Wanda is an encourager, a motivational and transformational speaker, image consultant, life coach and personal branding strategist. Her life is testament to the fact that it is never too late to pursue your dreams and redefine yourself! In her spare time, she enjoys volunteering with the local Dress for Success Chapter, contributing to her church's Career Ministry and baking. Wanda resides in Durham, North Carolina with her family.

FOURTEEN

Bottom of the Well: The Need for Self-Encouragement

Wanda Harris Pemberton

"Do you want to be happy? Learn the beautiful art of self-encouragement."—Sri Chinmoy

When most people envision a well, they conjure images of a dark, dank, scary place, with slick walls and no way out. My paternal grandmother, Almeater Drakeford Harris, had a well on her property, and for many years it was the only source of water for the family and the livestock she owned. When I think of that well, I remember the cool, sweet water it produced, not the danger or darkness associated with it. Sometimes wonderful things can come from the bottom of the well.

The well can be used as a metaphor for being in a dark place emotionally or spiritually. In those moments we may feel alone and lonely, but out of those moments can come sweet communion with God, clarity, and a renewed sense of purpose.

Stones from the Bottom of the Well

Many years ago wells were dug by hand and lined with stones. Those stones prevented the well from caving in on itself. If you were trying to escape from a well like that, you would probably try to find a way to use the stones for leverage. So think of a challenging time in your life – what "stones" did you use to free yourself from that situation? Prayer? Courage? Forgiveness? Try to list 4 "stones" that helped you lift yourself out of that emotional well:

1. _____

2. _____

3. _____

4. _____

We don't always have control over the difficulties that come into our lives; job loss, illness, the loss of a loved one, the end of a relationship are events which can be devastating to the spirit. However, our response to those events can greatly impact our ability to recover in a healthy way. Get into the habit of keeping "stones" in your pocket, so that you can keep yourself from staying in that emotional well for too long. The "stones" can be a favorite scripture, an affirmation or poem, or a picture of something or someone that brings you joy. Remember, the stones should be things that lift you up and out of a negative space.

Understanding Your Locus of Control

The term "locus of control" was originally coined by Julian Rotter, a noted psychologist and researcher. It refers to the way a person perceives the underlying causes of major life events. Some people have an internal locus of control, which means that they attribute their successes and failures to their personal choices, actions and efforts. Individuals with an external locus of control tend to attribute their successes and failures to things outside of their control (i.e. luck, fate, or other external circumstances).

How do you view the events in your life? Are you always a victim or are you able to find the victory in situations, even when they are challenging? Take this short quiz to determine whether you are operating from your internal locus of control, or if you are strongly influenced by external factors.

Place an "X" next to the statement you agree with the most.

	Statement A		Statement B	
1	I have a good chance of being promoted if I work hard and remain focused.		Success at work is a crap shoot – it's who you know that counts, nothing else matters.	

2	When I know I am right about something, I can persuade others to accept my point of view.		Trying to change someone's attitude is a waste of time, so why bother!	
3	I can learn how to get along with anyone.		It is impossible to please everybody, so why try?	
4	One person really can make a difference.		There is no way that one person can create a significant change in the world.	
5	I made some mistakes, but I refuse to be defined by my worst moment.		I don't want to put myself out there. I am sure everyone will remember what happened – nobody is going to give me a fair shot.	
7	My faith sustains me. I don't mind taking a chance on a new venture.		I decided not to try because none of my friends thought it was a good idea.	

Based on the article by Julian Rotter entitled, "Internal Control-External Control", originally printed in Psychology Today, 1971.

As you have probably figured out, the statements on the left reflect a perspective based on an "internal locus of control" – responses from a person who is taking ownership of their decisions and choices. The column on the right reflects a perspective based on an "external locus of control" – responses from a person who has been impacted and heavily influenced by external events.

When we think about the importance of self-encouragement, it is important to develop an internal locus of control. In other words, develop an attitude that says, (1) I may not have control over the circumstances, but I have control over my response to the circumstances; and (2) regardless of the outcome, I am alright with me.

A Word About Fear and Faith

Several years ago, I was going through difficult period in my personal life, and a good friend of mine told me that fear and faith could not exist in the same space. In other words, I could let my imagination run rampant with catastrophic thoughts of "what-ifs" or I could decide to deal with my issue head on, and trust that all of the things that were happening would result in a positive outcome (or at least a positive learning experience)for me, in the end. Turns out that my friend was right! I won't say it was an easy process, but I chose faith over fear, trust over trepidation, and persevered.

John Ortberg is the author of *If You Want to Walk on Water, You Have to Get Out of the Boat*. He uses the phrase "walking on water", to describe the process of pressing through fear and embracing the power and presence of God in your life. This work is relevant to the topic of self-encouragement because if you feel connected to God, you can rely on that connection when you are "in the well" and realize that you are never truly alone. The knowledge that you are connected to something bigger than yourself (whether you call it God, Jehovah, etc.), can provide you with an internal source of strength and the ability to encourage yourself.

John Orteberg also listed a number of characteristics essential to people who practice "walking on water":

1. Water-walkers recognize God's presence.

2. Water-walkers discern between faith and foolishness.

3. Water-walkers get out of the boat.

4. Water-walkers expect problems.

5. Water-walkers accept fear as the price of growth.

6. Water-walkers master failure management.

7. Water-walkers see failure as an opportunity to grow.

8. Water-walkers learn to wait on the Lord.

The Language of Self-Encouragement

To encourage someone is to acknowledge their effort – it is a conscious focus on the effort being made, rather than the actual outcome. The process of self-encouragement involves developing and maintaining a positive attitude, regardless of your circumstances. It means finding the "silver lining" in a circumstance and making a concerted effort to seek and find the positive elements (whatever they are), and not be overly focused on the negativity of the circumstance.

Self-encouragement does not mean you should ignore bad news or negative situations. We know that bad things can happen to anyone. However, the process of self-encouragement means making sure that the bad news does not take you into a negative spiral of self-talk (i.e.

things never work out for me, I always have bad luck, why do I keep trying, etc.). Instead of being self-critical or self-deprecating, we should use language that is affirming and positive – here are some examples:

Instead of Saying	Say to Yourself . . . . . .
I am so lazy/slow/bad at this.	I am trying to. . . .
Why should I bother?	I deserve this opportunity. I am going to learn how to . . . .
I can't do this.	I know I can . . . .
I am not making any progress.	I've gotten better at . . . .

Why Do I Need to Encourage Myself?

As important as is to have people around you who can offer support, prayers and encouragement, there comes a time when each of us find ourselves alone "in the well." In those moments – when no one else is around – we must find the internal strength (and desire) to climb out of that dark place. Les Brown, the famous motivational speaker and author, said, *"If you fall down, land on your back, because if you can look up, you can get up."*

When challenges and troubles come our way, we have to be able to pick ourselves up, and keep moving forward. When we give others the power to determine our mood, sense of self-worth, and value, our ability to function will be tempered by their whims and emotions. If your strength comes from within, you can weather storms, and you won't crumble when there is no one around to validate who you are and how much you are worth.

Think of a time when you were going through a challenging situation and no one was around – how did you recover?

_____

_____

_____

_____

_____

_____

What did you learn about yourself after that experience?

_____

_____

_____

_____

_____

_____

Survival Skills – What's in your tool bag?

Did you know that babies automatically hold their breath and begin moving their arms and legs in a paddling motion when they are placed face down in water? It's a reflex, an automatic response! As adults, we have to be in tune with our emotions so that we can generate a healthy response to challenges – a response that is automatic and not contingent upon external validation. In other words, you need to develop an internal reserve that automatically springs into action when you need to encourage yourself. Let's figure out what's in your internal reserve right now.

Rate yourself on a scale of 1 to 5 (with 1 being the least true and 5 being the most). There are no right or wrong answers, the quiz is designed to highlight what's in your reserve right now:

Acceptance	1	2	3	4	5
Anger Management	1	2	3	4	5
Gratitude	1	2	3	4	5
Willingness to Take Risk	1	2	3	4	5
The Ability to Forgive	1	2	3	4	5
Willingness to Start Over	1	2	3	4	5

How did you rate in each area? Were there areas which rated 3 or lower? If so, pick one and identify what would it take to get to 5?

_____

_____

_____

_____

_____

_____

_____

The Power of the Tongue

Ephraim Goodman, a linguist, is credited with connecting the phrase often associated with magical incantations – abracadabra, to the Aramaic phrase : Avra (which means I shall create) and Kedavra (which means as I say or speak).

Proverbs 18:21 (NIV) states, "*The tongue has the power of life and death, and those who love it will eat its fruit.*" So what does this mean for you? Both phrases acknowledge the powerful impact of our words, actions, and beliefs. The things we focus on are the things which become stronger, so if our focus is fixed on shortcomings, those deficiencies will steal our energy and our joy. Focusing on positive attributes does not negate the deficiencies, but allows us to use our energy in a more positive way. Practice speaking positivity into your circumstances, and reduce (or eliminate) negative self-talk.

Eight Easy Ways to Encourage Yourself

Remember your accomplishments – make a list and refer to it when necessary. Focus on your strengths and not your shortcomings – everyone is good at something, so spend more time utilizing your strengths.

1. **Balance self-criticism** – keeping it real is good, keeping it real negative is not. If you have a deficiency, acknowledge it, fix it (if necessary/possible), and move on.

2. **Expect a positive result** – if you start expecting to fail, you probably will. Develop confidence in your abilities.

3. **Practice resilience** – sometimes things just don't work out. Deal with it, but don't let the disappointment ground you permanently – try again or try something else.

4. **Meditate and pray** – regardless of the circumstances, your mind and spirit need to be at peace. Peace makes room for clarity and calm – everyone needs that to maintain balance.

5. **Give yourself permission to not be perfect** – nobody is perfect, so do your best and embrace your efforts.

6. **Get rid of negative self-talk** – sometimes we say things to ourselves that we would never say to another person. Stop putting yourself down, and stop giving other people permission to put you down. Celebrate your successes and know your worth.

7. **Spend time doing things that make you feel happy** – why spend all day doing things you don't enjoy, with people you don't like? Feed your passions and joy will follow.

8. **Make time to help others** – helping others is a great way to take your mind off of your own troubles. Remember, there is always someone who has not been as blessed as you have been.

We have come to the end of our journey, and I hope that you were able to find some "stones" you can use the next time you find yourself at the bottom of the well.

Recommended Reading

On Track, On Fire and On Purpose, by Barbara S. Talley

The Difference Maker, by John C. Maxwell

Designed for Success, by Dondi Scumaci

Battlefield of the Mind, by Joyce Meyers

If You Want to Walk on Water, You've Got to Get Out of The Boat, by John Ortberg

Positive Imaging: The Powerful Way to Change Your Life, by Norman Vincent Peale

Notes:

_____

_____

_____

_____

_____

_____

_____

_____

_____

_____

_____

_____

_____

_____

_____

_____

_____

_____

_____

_____

_____

_____

ABOUT THE AUTHOR

JERALYN B. MAJOR

Jeralyn B. Major, founder and executive director of Vision n View Consultants, a native of New Orleans, Louisiana is dedicated to helping women, girls, businesses, organizations and individuals turn their dreams into reality and to use their gifts, talents and skills to reach their full potential. Jeralyn has worked in retail, health care, and real estate prior to establishing her own consultant practice. With gifts of exhortation, leadership and administration she walks along side of and supports others in their efforts to live a more fulfilled life and to turn their dreams into reality.

Educated in the public school system of New Orleans, having attended Tulane University College, New Orleans Baptist Theological Seminary and currently attending Memphis Theological Seminary she is committed to acquiring the knowledge needed to impact the lives of others. She has worked hard to excel in any task or assignment that was given to her, affording her recognition and accolades including:

- A Quiet Hero – working behind the scenes to change her community and to touch lives.
- Emerging Voice – Women of the Storm
- Spirit of Excellence – presented by her peers as confirmation of her commitment to doing things with excellence.

As an advocate for spiritual, personal and professional growth and development, she believes that the potential to succeed is within all of us and that we are all valuable. Through her workshops, seminars, one on one counseling sessions, mentor opportunities and other informational settings, she has touched and empowered the lives of many.

She currently resides in Cordova, TN with her husband, Sidney H. Major, of 26 years. They are the parents of two adult children: Jowana Michelle Wilson and Sheldon Ashton Major.

Contact:
Jeralyn B. Major, Executive Director
Vision n View Consultants
visionnviewconsultants@gmail.com

FIFTEEN

Lessons Learned from My Mother

Jeralyn Major

I will begin this chapter by being very transparent. This was not my first option in chapter choices; it was actually my third! While it was not *my* first choice, it was *God's* first choice, and so it is that I am writing to share with you the many valuable lessons I have learned from my mother.

I could probably fill several pages with a grocery list of the things my mother told and showed me during my youth. I didn't think when she was imparting these gifts that I would need them to be able to navigate through life. But as I grew and things began to happen in my life, I was thankful to be able to recall many of the words, the stories and the examples she taught and shared.

I am going to share a story with you that helps me to put into words and acknowledge all of the lessons I learned from my mother. In my thirties, my mother presented me with a beautiful ceramic eagle statue and today it sits on my desk as a reminder of the day that my mother said to me, *"J, you are my eagle child."* You may wonder what is so special about that statement. Well, walk with me through the pages of this chapter as I try to explain and share what it means to be an eagle child/person. Some facts about the eagle help to paint the picture. The eagle is a majestic bird, strong, resilient and for those of us in the United States, it is our national bird. Now when my mother said those words to me, remember I said I was in my thirties, which meant she was in her fifties.

My mother lost her mother at the age of 9, leaving her upbringing to grandparents, aunts, uncles and other relatives; they all did a good job. However, for most of my childhood I don't recall my mother being very vocal in expressing her feelings, but rather demonstrative. So when she verbalized to me that I was her eagle child, that penetrated a deep place inside of me. All I could think about was how amazing it was that my mother thought of me as an eagle. Why so amazing, you ask? Because in all my years growing up I knew my mother loved me and I knew she was preparing me for something greater, but knowing what is written and said about an eagle and knowing that she could see that in me and to say it to me was wonderful. At thirty, my mother described me as her *eagle child*, but between the ages of ten to fifteen, she described me as her *sassy child* because I always had something to say and always tried to get my point across. (Things haven't changed much!)

As I began to think about how I would start this chapter, this particular story was the first idea that came to my mind. Now, the thought that immediately followed was that ***I learned how to be an eagle from my mother.*** I did not realize or even think about it when she said it to me some 20+ years ago, but today as I think about those words and look back over my life, I can boldly proclaim that I learned to be an eagle from my mother, which has sustained and propelled me throughout life. From time to time, I would reflect on what my mother said and the things my mother did. Even today, in crowded rooms with other women, I have often used and have heard others use many of the stories that my momma and their mothers said. As you are reading, I am sure you can recall some of the things that your mother used to say, so let's take a few moments and make a list.

What your momma told you: (sayings and lessons)

1. _____

2. _____

3. _____

4. _____

5. _____

After completing your list, invite a friend to do a list, as well. Compare the list and you may find that you have a lot in common and that you use some of the same sayings/lessons in raising your children and living your life. A second step with the list is to think about, reflect and discuss with your friend how the things on the list have helped to shape your life. As a rule, I never ask anyone to do something that I would not do so following is the list compiled by my sister Eugenia, daughter Jowana, son Sheldon, friend Marilyn Smith and her sisters. Compare our list to yours. Have fun with this and use it with your co-workers, women's group, your daughter's friends or any other gathering of women that you are associated with, young or old, as it is a good sisterhood moment!

Famous Sayings of Hope E. Smith

1. *"…look it up in the dictionary!"*

    Whenever we wanted to know the spelling or definition of one of my mother's million dollar words, her response was always for us to look it up in the dictionary. She would make us sound it out phonetically and read her the definition and spelling.

2. *"I'll kill you! Call the police and tell them I did it!"*

    She had to be really angry to use this one. Of course we had to have done something REALLY wrong and we probably needed the police to save us!

3. *"What's the moral of the story?"* or *"Is it highly moral or religious?"*

    This one we used to hate. This line would come during and after every movie, TV show, or request to see a movie. Sometimes you would just ask yourself the question and then get out of notion.

4. *"There will be two licks passed, I'm going to hit you and you are going to hit the floor!"*

    (This was on my list as well, but with a slightly different meaning.) This is the line we would get when we were really in trouble and discipline was delayed intentionally. At this point, she was too angry to discipline immediately and the quiet storm had become a tornado!

Ms. Gloria's meaning - If during the process of being disciplined you ever got the crazy notion to take a stand, this was a reminder of what would happen.

5. *"...turn around!"*

This is the message that would come on a note from the ushers in church from the back row where my mother would be sitting. We would be so afraid to turn around, but when we did, she would roll those eyes and all the talking would cease until after church.

In Ms. Gloria's words (my mother)

6. *"Call the police, it's a ride down and a walk back!"*

Translation – I am going to discipline you one way or another and if I get in trouble so be it once.

7. *"Don't take any wooden nickels!"*

Translation – don't let anyone make a fool of you.

8. *"Let sleeping dogs lie!"*

Translation – don't bring up dead things, and some things are better left as they were.

Earlier I eluded to the fact that my mother described me as her eagle child. This is not to say that my other siblings do not possess the same traits, but I think what Momma was saying was, of all of her children (six of us total) those traits were most dominant and most expressed in me. When we have family gatherings or when my sisters and I talk, it is quite clear that they have learned some of the same lessons from my mother and that we are all better because of those lessons.

Today the eagle is lifted as a model for leadership. Well, from where I sit and in thinking about my life and the lessons my mother taught - **the eagle is a model for living.**

The eagle is known for its vision - its ability to see great distances and to look directly into the sun without being blinded.

Lesson #1 – Look Beyond

My mother taught me to look beyond what was right in front of me - to see something different and not to lose focus because of what I might see. She also taught me to work hard to move towards what is in the distance. She also taught me that in looking forward, don't just leap but prepare for it by positioning myself to move closer and closer to that which lies ahead.

It is also said that eagles never eat dead meat.

Lesson #2 – Don't take advantage of a dead or dying situation.

(It is also said that eagles never eat dead meat.) Don't hurt others who are already wounded and don't steal someone else's prize. Work hard for what you want - save, prepare and store up. Help those who are down and share what you have with those who are less fortunate. (A third trait of an eagle is the ability to find and fly in storms.)

Lesson #3 – Face challenges head on.

Do not run from the challenges that come in life. Even when you find yourself in a difficult situation, face it head on. Learn from the challenge and use it to catapult yourself to another level.

And the fourth and final point that I want to offer is that eagles are very gentle and attentive to their young.

Lesson #4 – Take care of the young and the young at heart.

Looking back over my childhood, I don't think I would use the world gentle in describing my mother when it came to raising her children. Being a single mother of six, she had to show us who was in control and that she ruled the roost. Yet like the eagle (known for its ferocity, gentleness and attentiveness to its young), so was my mother in her own way. I remember my mother putting her children first, always making certain we had what we needed, and in many cases what we wanted, as well. I know you think that is the norm, but in many cases it is not. Case in point: children grow fast and as a result have constant needs for clothing and other accessories. Well, year after year (as the need arose) my brothers, sisters and I got new coats, while I remember my mother wearing the same winter coat season after season. She would find a way to mend it, wearing extra clothes underneath as the coat became thinner and thinner. That was only one situation I lifted as an example of how my mother taught me to put your children first. What is more interesting is that I watched my mother apply the same principle to other children in the neighborhood when she brought food, snacks, treats (or staples if someone else was in need). She always made a point to share with them, expecting nothing in return. Another thing I can recall from my youth had to do with the fact that my mother opened our home as a haven for the children in the community. My oldest sister was the social butterfly in the family, always participating in everything. On those occasions when there was a need for a location to gather (for whatever reason), my mother always made our home available and provided refreshments while serving as a safe haven so that the other mothers could feel comfortable and assured that their children were being watched over.

While this list is not exhaustive, what has been lifted as lessons from my mother can be applied and adapted in many situations. One thing I heard my mother saying over and over as we were growing was this: "No man is an island! You can't live in this world alone and as sure as you are living, we all need somebody." I'll close the chapter with those words and offer them as a guide for living in this world today. Treat everyone with respect, kindness and compassion and the same will come back to you.

Notes:

_____

_____

_____

_____

_____

_____

_____

_____

_____

_____

_____

_____

_____

_____

_____

_____

_____

_____

_____

_____

_____

_____

ABOUT THE AUTHOR

Pastor Cheryl Minter

Pastor Cheryl Minter is a mother of three young adults: Stacey, Brittany and Jeremy. She is an author, conference speaker, and Certified Empowerment and Spiritual Life Coaching.

Cheryl Minter is the Sr. Pastor of Anointed Word Life Center in Fayetteville, Georgia under the leadership of Bishop Dianne R. Collins. Pastor Minter holds a B.S. in Education from Tennessee State University.

She is a Certified Empowerment & Spiritual Life Coaching from Rehema International School of Coaching Alliance: visit Pastor Cheryl Minter's website at www.movingfclc.com.

SIXTEEN

I Was Not Built To Break

Cheryl Minter

First let me start by saying this story that I am about to tell is about me, about accountability and staying on the path that God created for me! The word of God says that before *I formed thee, I knew thee;* the word 'knew' implies that God himself had conversation with me (and you) before the beginning of time. God already knew what would take place in our lives. He knows everything about us; there is nothing hidden and nothing is a surprise to him. It's hard to believe that a loving and gentle God would care so much about me (us), even from the very beginning, His mercy and grace are so profound that he knew what I would do ,what I would say, how I would treat people, yet he still wanted and needed me. That's the kind of God I (we) serve.

Even before birth I was supposed to be aborted as my mother had a large tumor that was pressing against me as a baby in utero and the doctor suggested that she should abort because if she continued with the pregnancy there was a possibility that I would die and she would lose her life. BUT God has another plan. My mother believes in the power of prayer and the word of God so she declared that if God saw fit to cause her to get pregnant he would see to it that she would deliver. As you can tell I'm here, but I lived in an incubator for about 6 weeks as I was born premature. .But once I got the hang of living there was no turning back. I had to learn to fight at an early age and what I didn't understand like so many people is God has ordained for some of us to become fighters and to stand strong for those that can't or don't know how to fight for themselves. What I mean concerning my fight is that I learned the art of prayer and became an intercessor, the one that stands in the gap for others.

As a child I was rejected and felt betrayed by others (not my immediate family members) and as a child you want to feel accepted by your peers, and not feel the pain of rejection that so often led to insecurity, .so I began to excel in sports as it lessened the pain of the being rejected, feeling insecure. I would do just about anything else that help avoid the devil from lifting its head to breath havoc in my life. See the devil knows just what to use against you to try and cause you not to fulfill destiny. If you don't love yourself how can anyone else love you! We find something (drugs alcohol, relationship business, jobs,) that will fill the void and release the pain so we won't have to think about what's going on with us at that point in time. .Little did I know that playing sports would set the needed discipline , rules, boundaries of team play, sportsmanship (character building) into my life that I would need later to complete the task at hand that God had called me to do. I learn to fight through pain to press forward to victory.

Early in life I learned to deal with disappointment but more importantly how to handle the pain ,emotions and the storms of life, The challenges that were handed me were created to kill me but God was using it as a training ground for his purpose. All things work together for your good and according to his purpose (Rom 8:28)

I had loving parents that taught us as children that God is our source of strength and our salvation in order to bend and not break which requires you to walk in forgiveness, with ones self and others.

Forgiveness isn't easy. Believe me I have tried from personal experiences and have been successful after several failed attempts. Yes, I attempted to walk in my own strength after knowing what God's word said and tried to forgive the person that hurt me but to no avail . When I saw that person again either I would go the opposite way or I would pretend to not see them. Well, that's not what God had in mind when he wanted us to forgive. What we fail to understand is that when we won't forgive we are really hurting ourselves not the other person. From my own experience I learn that most of the time the other person has moved on with their life as we struggle with the pain, hurt and disappointment that has occurred in our lives. The funniest thing is when they see us they can't even remember what offense has taken place. So it would be better if we quickly forgive and move forward with our lives rather than staying stuck in a position that takes away the authority, peace, comfort, and love that God has ordained for each of us to have.

Phillipians (amp) 4:13 reminds us that we can do whatever we need to do with God's power.

I was so disappointed when I ended up getting a divorce. I couldn't believe that two people who were called and chosen couldn't make a marriage work. All I could see was the way he treated me,; the verbal abuse was too much to handle. I wasn't equipped for the way I was being handled.. I had lost touch with my soul and I had lost sight of my dream (without a vision the people perish) and I really thought that this would be the end of me with nowhere to go and no one to turn to. But if you ever step out of the will of God ,you will run into the enemy's camp and get dealt with, because no matter what you desire, if it is not the will of God you have crossed over into the enemy's territory..God is able to protect you and keep you from death, but you my friend have opened up the door for some things that weren't a part of God's plan to be within your life.

The hand writing was on the wall as I was in love and my emotions were outweighing what God had spoken to me; my flesh was longing for something I couldn't handle..Then on top of all that I made statements that God had never showed me or told me anything different. I was mad at God! Yes, you read it right. I felt betrayed by God that he would allow this to happen to me after all I was preaching and praying. But in spite of my pain I want to let you know the word of God is true because before destruction God always send a warning!! He did but I ignored all the signs of the warnings from God and his messengers because I wanted what I wanted.

Oh, My God, I began to cry and God began to reveal something about me and how I was insecure and how since my mother had died I felt alone and thought that I had nobody. That was the biggest lie ever spoken to me. So I put myself in a needy place, instead of trusting in the true and the living God. How can you love someone else when you can't love your own self. One must always value oneself before anyone else will because then you will not allow someone else to mistreat you or devalue what you bring to the table. If any person can't see your value and respect what you have to offer, then no matter what you say or do, they really refuse to see who you are! They have to see you on their own. The disappointment lasted for several years in the marriage because I felt in my heart I was a roommate AND a mother to my husband because of the position I placed myself in as a caregiver. Then slowly I started to disrespect him as a man and a minister. Need I tell you that all kinds of emotion began to flood my heart, mind and spirit.

I believed in my heart of hearts that this man was the one from God, not saying he wasn't but he wasn't *at the time.* Out of time is not God's perfect time for any of us! The devil beat me and I beat myself alone with his verbal abuse because after a minute(within a month of marriage) I knew I was out of the will of God, but I was determine to make it work because after all we were both saved ,ministers and I could pray!! How many of you know I went on the adventure for a life time, but because God is so loving and merciful he wouldn't allow the enemy to kill me ; he could only bend me for such a time as this! I didn't come to tear anyone down just to expose the enemy and to say all of us make mistakes in our lives but if we are willing to admit our part in what happened God will squeeze the bitterness ,hurt, pain, disappointment out of us and allow our story to become his glory.

Yes I am here to tell you if you let it go and move ahead that better things are set in motion for you to accomplish and better days are ahead. Now this wasn't an easy task because I had to make up in my mind to forgive him and myself. Every day I strove to be at peace with what had happened. As I began to read and study the word of God , I made a decision to live it! It will do you no good if you don't plan to carry out what you learned because, just as we learn a skill on a job, we must also learn to apply God's word in our life in the same manner. That's one of the reasons God sent Jesus as,he came to show us how to live a holy life, to carry out the very nature and plan of God and the Holy Spirit that would enable us to walk in forgiveness.

God word reveals to us how harmful it is to live with unforgiveness and the power behind forgiving someone.Forgiveness is not you doing that person a favor because you are doing yourself a favor by releasing that person and allowing God to repay. God said that vengeance is mine and I will repay.The results of forgiving people is that you release the hurt, pain, bitterness, and anger inside of yourself and you are able to live with joy and unspeakable peace that surpasses.the other person, and the devil gets confused because it was supposed to have a different effect!

I just wanted to share with you that in order for you to live an overcoming life and a life of victory you must wrap your heart and mind around forgiveness. I just want to share a couple of things I did that helped me to navigate through the storms of life . Please know I have had so many events and people that tried to break me, from the death and loss of my mom, 3 brothers, and 2 sisters all within a time span of about 5 years . I thought I would lose it until God spoke to my heart and commanded peace to be still because if I lost my mind I would never fulfill the promises of God concerning my life. You must know that the enemy is coming against your mind and your peace so that the very thing God promised, you can't have BUT God is well able to keep those that belongs to him. There are many people that are married or were married to a minister or a saved man/woman of God but don't know how to deal with the aftermath of the pain and the hurt during that relationship; I have dealt with this from first- hand experience. I believe God is using this type of mishap to help others from being stuck so they can move forward in life. It's all in your perception and your choices.

Forgiveness is the foundation of thrusting you forward into a brighter future filled with peace and joy and satisfaction in every area of your life.

1. First I had to make a quality decision that forgiveness was God's best for me. If God could forgive me my sins and trespasses then I was able and equipped to forgive others. I knew that when someone viewed me and couldn't understand why I would forgive them that I could still walk in love towards them which is priceless.

2. I learn to quickly depend upon God when I needed to forgive because sometimes my emotions said no we are not doing this again! But my heart knew.I needed to do this for me. God will give you the strength to forgive if that's what you want to do and he will give you the grace to see it through.

3. Next I had to understand my actions and reactions; .my actions allow me to not act like Christ and my emotions were all over the place with getting mad and wanting to handle the person myself. But my reaction allowed me to step aside, get my feeling in check and make the wises choice concerning myself without having to ask God to forgive me and the person. I could make the right choice to do what was right in the sight of God.

4. I would pray for them. Now this is easier said than done until you make the decision that your flesh is not going to be the boss of you, but God's word will always lead you and guide you into what is best for you. **Matt5:44(amp) Jesus teaches us to love our enemies and pray for those who persecute you.** Remember it s for you not them. I have learned that when I do something nice for the person that has wronged me that it's like pouring heaps of coals on their head because they just can't understand why you did what you did. Sometimes I didn't understand it either but I have seen the power of God move and it is such a humbling experience and the power of his love is unimaginable.

The choice is always your choice to do what is right in the sight of God and to overcome evil with good. Forgiveness is always the better choice. I survived one of my darkest hours. I wasn't built to break. I work off of God's strength according to his word, **I can do all things through Christ who strengthen me. (Phil 4:13)**

I had to conform to the image of Christ; God wants each of us to be Christ-occupied. But the Bible tells us that in our flesh dwells **no** good **thing (Romans 7:18), and that we should put no confidence in our flesh (Philippians 3:3)**. It is God's desire that we look like him. We must mirror the image; the attitude and likeness of Christ. How do we do that? By meditating and declaring what he said, believing everything he said, and as we see ourselves like him we behold his beauty. We do this by the spirit of the lord.

But we all, with unveiled face, beholding as in a mirror the glory of the Lord, are being transformed into the same image from glory to glory, just as by the Spirit of the Lord. —2 Corinthians 3:18

The best way to change yourself is to forget self and be occupied with Christ. When you read the word of God, see His beauty, His glory, His compassion and His grace. See him as you keep meditating on His greatness. The Holy Spirit will begin to work inside you. He will transform you into the very image of Christ. You will be changed from glory to glory, experiencing true and lasting inward transformation! Behold the woman in the mirror who's reflection is just like Jesus! It's possible and each of us have been called to do it. Who are you beholding in the mirror? yourself (flesh) or Jesus (spirit).Forgiveness is a gift that God offers so we cannot only change ourselves but those around us.

Hang in there Help is on the way!! God is our helper. We really can trust God to help us in any situation and any circumstances. Yes we can. We can always agree with the word and apply the word to our everyday life. Truth be told God really wants to help us in every situation no matter how bad it appears to us. We should always trust that he has our better or best interest at hand, no need to worry ,fret ,fear or get overwhelmed. The holy Spirit which is our helper in life wants to help us move into the greater life that has been plan for us. Jeremiah 29:11 says 'for I know the thoughts that I think toward you, saith the lord, thoughts of peace and not evil, to give you an expected end.' God has several thoughts toward you and what that implies is if one plan that's connected to someone else doesn't work then let try something different. We are all given free will; you can't make someone do or be something they don't want to be regardless if God spoke it. Free will. God is saying move forward. Move to something greater and if it doesn't yield peace move forward .God is not the author of confusion. He wants to give you an expected end…what do you expect? Peace. Freedom, victory , healing, wholeness, happiness ,love, joy? This is what God wants for you.

The Holy Spirit will never push anything on you for he is gentle and kind ; what he has to offer should never be refused. He is the one that knows the answer to every problem and will help you through each one . He is waiting for you to ask for his help. Every problem you have matters to God. *God is not holding out on you.* Jesus said in John 15:5 (NIV), "Apart from me you can do nothing." And that's so true. God is not holding out on you; He actually likes it when we ask for His help You and I have so many opportunities to feel sad or discouraged and have a bad attitude, but God wants us to stay strong in Him. Those who do will eventually come out on top, because there's no way the enemy can hold you back if you will trust God and keep your hope in Him.

When you're hurting, in trouble, or waiting on an answer, you need to believe that your help has been sent and it is on the way. God may not come when you want it, but it will be there right on time and on God's calendar. Help is on the way.

No matter what your circumstances look like or what the world may say, hang in there because help is on the way! While you are waiting give yourself permission to bend but not break!

Notes:

ABOUT THE AUTHOR

GLORIA THOMAS ANDERSON, LMSW

Gloria is a licensed, master's degree social educator, inspirational author and motivational speaker. Her own story of a near-death experience from a life-threatening illness gives encouragement and inspires many patients, families and caregivers across the country.

Gloria teaches, develops and facilitates customized cultural diversity training workshops for healthcare, mental health and social service professionals in the areas of grief and loss, end-of-life care and spirituality.

She is the sole author of "The African-American Spiritual and Ethical Guide to End-of-Life Care", first written in 2006 as a research paper that received funding to become a patient educational resource. She presented her work at the North American International Conference on Spirituality and Social Work in Ontario, Canada that same year.

Gloria has authored several cultural competency-training manuals and her popular inspirational, self-help book, Passion For Your Purpose: Discovering Peace, Direction and Balance in Your Life is in its second publication.

Additionally, she is the creative energy of authentic inspirational gifts and prints through Heart Tones™ (www.hearttones.com). She is also a licensed minister whose faith empowers her to advocate and help others on their life journey of purpose. She is affectionately known as "The Inspirational Advisor" from her online column, "Inspiring Insights for Your Soul & Spirit!"

On a personal note, Gloria is the mother of two grown daughters and the grandmother of five. She enjoys playing her keyboard, taking leisurely walks and writing (of course!).

Contact:
Gloria Thomas Anderson, LMSW
Heart Tones
P. O. Box 32731
Kansas City, MO 64171
(913) 433-3877
Email: gloria@hearttones.com
Website: www.hearttones.com

SEVENTEEN

Out of the Darkness, Into the Light

*"God's second chances are innumerable grace opportunities
to accomplish His Purpose in your life".*
—Gloria Thomas Anderson

Gloria Thomas Anderson

My story may be different from your story, and yet they are alike in that the chapters of life consist of three universal commonalities we all share: we are all born, we live, and then we die. All that happens in life produces change. Change is our common ally. No one lives without it. The scripts of life are different, but the fact remains that whether we have little or much, pain or joy, justice or none—we breathe the same air in life and we share the same earth in death.

Second chances come to remind us that our lives are not our own. As you look back over your life, do you ever think about the second chances you may have had over the years? What about having the chance to start over again after an unsuccessful relationship or business venture? I remember talking with a man once who told me that he had missed the chance to raise his first child because of his reckless lifestyle, but later in life had another child in a second marriage, giving him the chance to be a responsible, loving father. Someone else I met in the hospital shared how kidney failure saved his life after a long addiction to drugs and alcohol led to dialysis. *"God gave me a second chance"*, he said at the close of our brief conversation.

There are so many examples of life's second chances and you can probably think of a few of your own. I too, can think of countless times that God has given me new opportunities to correct, change or consider something different. But the second chance I received after a near death experience is one I will never forget.

When I was first diagnosed with a life-threatening illness, numbness and fear seized my soul. Although I had not felt well for nearly a year, I innately sensed something was wrong, but my doctor insisted that the problem was related to hereditary high blood pressure. Even while taking multiple medications to control the blood pressure, it continued to get higher.

My second chance began one Friday morning when I thought I was having a heart attack and drove myself to the ER. After two days in the hospital and multiple medical tests, a tumor was found on my left adrenal gland. Surgery was recommended right away.

My doctors seemed confident that I would be okay once the tumor was removed, but the reality was quite the opposite after the surgery. Complications arose that were not expected or explainable. My condition worsened as the doctors fervently sought to find answers. *What went wrong? Why wasn't I getting better? Was God calling me home?*

These were just a few of the many racing thoughts that flooded my mind. I couldn't understand why my vitals wouldn't stabilize and neither could my doctors.

In times like these, logical and rational intellectualism can go right out the window. Real life situations can sometimes defy natural reasoning. Such was the case here. I'll never forget the days that led up to my near death experience. All I could think about was my children and grandchildren and how much I would miss them.

As I lay on what I thought was my bed of transition to heaven's glory, I could feel and smell the presence of Death in my room. For two days, the fearful stench remained lurking in the atmosphere, reminding me in every waking moment that it was waiting for the green light to take me into eternity. Deep inside, I knew that I was dying and the thought gripped me with incredible fear and trembling. No one could stop the impeding end of what I had known as "my life". No one human, that is. I realize now how fragile life really is. One day you can be up, healthy and moving—the next unable to function, completely dependent on others.

I remember becoming weaker and weaker. My blood pressure and heart rate rose higher and higher and my potassium level remained way too low. I held on to the Word of God and kept my bible opened to scripture verses, 1 Peter 2:24 and Isaiah 53:5.

I would lay those open bible pages on my stomach and say in my mind, *"By His stripes, I am healed"*...

> Isaiah 53:5—*"But he was wounded for my transgressions, he was bruised for my iniquities: the chastisement of our peace was upon him; and with his stripes I am healed."*
>
> 1 Peter 2:24—*"Who his own self bore our sins in his own body on the tree, that we, being dead to sins, should live unto righteousness; by whose stripes ye were healed."*

If there ever was a moment to put total trust in God, this was that moment. Although the surgery successfully removed the tumor, my body continued to weaken. Fear gripped me as thoughts of dying consumed my mind. Suddenly, another bible scripture flashed in my mind that immediately caused me to stop fighting against death:

For we walk by faith, not by sight; We are confident, I say, and willing rather to be absent from the body, and to be present with the LORD".
—2 Corinthians 5: 7-8

I had read this verse many times, but something about it made it real as I surrendered to God in my frailness. Revelation of its' powerful truth resonated within me and my soul rejoiced! *"I win! I win either way!"* If I continue to have life on earth or if I leave this earthly body to be with the Lord—I win!"

> *For we know that if our earthly house of this tabernacle were dissolved, we have a building of God, an house not yet made with hands, eternal in the heavens.* —2Corinthians 5:1

Barely able to move, now sensing the end was near, I closed my eyes and yielded to Death. I made the conscious choice in my heart to flow with God's will rather than fight against it. As I dosed off into what I thought was eternal sleep, I saw an indescribably beautiful brightness of light that began to draw me into it. Right before entering, an image appeared blocking the way, which was a large white poster with huge, black letters that read, "NO!" Surprised, I barely opened my eyes, softly saying the word, "No?" as a question, when the Spirit of God spoke to my heart and said, *"NO! I will restore you."*

God communicates with each of us differently because we are unique individuals. God often speaks to me visually through pictures, words and language, which can be primary tools in the lives of creative souls. Almost immediately, I began to get stronger.

Within 24 hours, my vitals stabilized and the normal functionality of my body occurred miraculously. Although I was able to leave the hospital shortly after that, the side effects from medications caused me to wind up back in the hospital several more times in the next three months. I continued to hold to my confession of healing in spite of these natural circumstances. Everything visible—the lab results, my fluctuating vital signs, and even the doctors' assessment of the situation—contradicted my confession. I knew that regardless of what was happening in the reality, I was healed and the manifestation would come in God's time. I chose to believe God over the circumstances of what I felt, what I was seeing, and what I was hearing.

Your faith will be tested. Regardless of what happens in life, holding on to God's word is imperative to experience the power of God. Revelation from God often transcends evidence-based research or intellectual knowledge. Some truths are only known through living faith, by believing and trusting in God. Some truths will never be explained through human thought or reasoning.

God is not limited by the finiteness of man and science, for God is Infinite in wisdom, knowledge and understanding. God determines our life course—when we are born and when we will die. No one else has the power to create life and then return it to its own earth from which it came.

Psalm 145:3-4 reads, *"Do not put your trust in princes nor in a human being, in whom there is no help. His Spirit departs, he returns to his earth; In that very day his plans perish."*

My time to remain on the earth was extended by God Almighty, The Creator of Life. My earthly assignment had not yet been completed. I knew that God was in control and knowing this supernatural truth gave me a calm sense of peace that 'all is well' through the challenging months of recovery that ensued.

God continued to communicate with me through simple language; the word, "Restoration", remained a constant reminder in my thoughts. His promise to restore me reached the depths of my being—physically, emotionally and spiritually. I began to confess daily, *"I am restored."*

During those three months, I was unable to take care of myself and required assistance with daily living activities, such as, bathing, eating, and walking. Yet, I knew without a doubt that God's spoken word to me of restoration was forthcoming. Again, recognizing that faith is an unseen reality yet to be revealed.

My youngest daughter came to care for me on her vacation. She looked up the word, "restore" and proceeded to type the meanings of the word on the computer and brought it to my bedside. I framed it and to this very day it serves as a reminder that God did just what He said. *(See picture below)*

RESTORE v. *renew; bring back; fix, recondition, rejuvenate, revive, refresh, put in good repair, rehabilitate, regenerate*

The promises of God are Yea and Amen. My divine healing is a miracle and I know that God healed my body and restored my life when death was imminent—even expected by some. The experience of divine healing comes from the Greek word "Sozo", which means, *"to heal, save, make well or whole"*. God cancelled my appointment with eternity. I no longer fear death because I understand that when our lives are hid in Christ, we will live again.

God is the Giver of life and The Eternal Decision-Maker. God decides when death comes, not people or situations. We don't leave here until God says so.

Second chances in the wake of death's shadow can be life changing. Petty frustrations, negative relationships, and other things that used to be major distractions become minor in the big picture of life.

Second chances to come out of dark places are not always related to illness, dying or death. Our lives may have other kinds of darkness that come through real life circumstances and situations. That darkness could be experiencing divorce, losing a loved one, going through financial struggles or battling with depression, among many other things. In fact, darkness can be *anything* that interferes with the Light of Jesus shining in and through *you*. Darkness *cannot* exist when light is present.

> *"For with thee is the fountain of life; in thy light shall we see light."*
> —Psalm 36:9
>
> *"Thy word is a lamp unto my feet and a light unto my path."*
> —Psalm119:105

Having the simple capabilities to breathe, move and think are second chance gifts we all get every day we are alive. God has no respect of persons and has all power to restore and renew as He pleases. We don't have to understand it, we just have to receive and believe God, regardless of what comes in life and regardless of the outcomes. Second chances are really the countless graces of God in our lives on the earth.

God loves us with an everlasting love that cannot be measured or explained by rational human intelligence. As long as we have breath, we have new chances to do and be what God has ordained for our lives. Understanding that the power of God resides within you is key to surviving those most troubling and fearful life moments. Life happens sometimes in peculiar ways—turns…twists—twists and turns—that can shift your sight away from Light. Trust God *more* in those times. Believe God anyway, regardless of what and how situations appear.

Allow the knowing of Almighty God's presence to guide you gently back to His pasture. You may not understand the "whys" or be able to make sense of the darkness. You may have questions that seem to lack answers or reason. Remember, you are not alone in the dark seasons of your life. God is always present.

In our brokenness, God recreates us. Just like newly enlisted men and women coming into the Army are required to abandon their own ways of doing things to be rebuilt as soldiers, so is it with the people of God. We must be transformed by the renewing of our minds and become new creations in Christ Jesus. It is a life-long process of becoming more and more light in a lost and dark world.

By releasing our "whys" and "what ifs", we can position ourselves to receive more truth and light through our relationship with God through Jesus Christ by the power of the Holy Spirit. Life is a beautiful and valuable gift of God to hold dear. Every breath comes from God. God is The Source of all sustenance and being.

The miraculous recovery from a life-threatening disease was my second chance to continue the course that God ordained from the foundations of the earth. God gives all of us second chance seasons throughout our lives. Those innumerable grace opportunities come in order for us to do His Will and fulfill His Purpose. God's Grace is immediate with absolute certainty in any painful situation life brings. Calm serenity returns in the midst of valley times when we yield to God. The circumstance you face may be challenging beyond belief, but with God, there is no need to fret or fight. We can face trying situations when we know that God is with us and that we are never alone, no matter how alone we may feel.

When you go through storms in life and come through still standing, consider it a second chance. That second chance can be a way to let you know that God is not through with you yet!

No matter what is going on in your life, remember that it's not over 'til it's over. Second chances are life's little miracles waiting to shower us with sprinkles of hope and courage. May you choose to keep moving forward by faith toward the eternal Light of God in your season of a second chance.

> *For God, who commanded the light to shine out of darkness, hath shone in our hearts, to give the light of the knowledge of the glory of God in the face of Jesus Christ.* —2 Corinthians 4:6

Second Chance Prayer:

God, I thank You for the blessing of second chances. You are the Giver of Life and because of You, I have life. I ask for wisdom to make wise choices and to do those things You are calling me to do in this season. Thank you for completing the work in me through the Spirit. I yield to You, O Lord, and know by faith that all things are working together for my good because I love You and I am called according to Your purpose. I give all the glory, praise and honor to You. Amen.

Notes:

_____

_____

_____

_____

_____

_____

_____

_____

_____

_____

_____

_____

_____

_____

_____

_____

_____

_____

_____

_____

_____

THE PROFESSIONAL WOMAN NETWORK
Training and Certification on Women's Issues

Linda Ellis Eastman, President & CEO of The Professional Woman Network, has trained and certified over two thousand individuals to start their own consulting/seminar business. Women from such countries as Brazil, Argentina, the Bahamas, Costa Rica, Bermuda, Nigeria, South Africa, Malaysia, and Mexico have attended trainings.

Topics for certification include:
• Diversity & Multiculturalism
• Women's Issues
• Women: A Journey to Wellness
• Save Our Youth
• Teen Image & Social Etiquette
• Leadership & Empowerment Skills for Youth
• Customer Service & Professionalism
• Marketing a Consulting Practice
• Professional Coaching
• Professional Presentation Skills

If you are interested in learning more about becoming certified or about starting your own consulting/seminar business contact:

The Professional Woman Network
P.O. Box 333
Prospect, KY 40059
(502) 566-9900
lindaeastman@prodigy.net
www.prowoman.net

Women's Empowerment Series

The Empowered Woman: Purpose, Passion & Possibilities

The POWER of Transformation: Reinventing Your Life

Baby Boomers: Secrets for Life After 50!

The Female Leader: Empowerment, Confidence & Passion

What's the Difference? Embracing Diversity & Inclusivity

The Young Professional Woman: Breaking Into the Business World & Succeeding

A View from the Top: Exceptional Leadership Strategies

Getting Well: Mind, Body & Spirit

How to Break the Glass Ceiling Without a Hammer

Breaking Free: Overcoming Self-Sabotage

Creating a Blueprint for Inner Change: Tools for Personal Growth

How to Survive When Your Ship is Sinking: Weathering Life's Storms

Leaders in Pearls: How to Be a Change Architect

Celebration of Life: Inspiration for Women

Releasing Strongholds: Letting Go of What's Holding You Back

The Power of a Woman: Embracing the Woman Within

The Power of Change: Reinvent Yourself at Any Age

Life is an Attitude. The Power of Positive Thinking

Transformation: Reinventing the Woman Within

The Self-Architect: Redesigning Your Life

Becoming Your Own Best Friend

The Woman's Handbook for Self-Empowerment

Remove the Mask! Living an Authentic Life

The Woman's Handbook for Self-Confidence

A Journey Within: Self-Discovery for Women

Learning to Love Yourself: Self-Esteem for Women

The African American Library

Sister to Sister A Guide for African American Girls
Bruised But Not Broken
Learning to Love Yourself: A Handbook for the African American Woman
Wellness for the African American Woman: Mind, Body & Spirit
Life Skills for the African American Woman
Raising African American Boys
Raising African American Girls
Living Your Vision and Purpose

The Professional Woman Network - Book Series

Becoming the Professional Woman
Customer Service & Professionalism for Women
Self-Esteem & Empowerment for Women
The Young Woman's Guide for Personal Success
The Christian Woman's Guide for Personal Success
Survival Skills for the African-American Woman
Overcoming the SuperWoman Syndrome
You're on Stage! Image, Etiquette, Branding & Style
Women's Journey to Wellness: Mind, Body & Spirit
A Woman's Survival Guide for Obstacles, Transition & Change
Women as Leaders: Strategies for Empowerment & Communication
Beyond the Body! Developing Inner Beauty
The Young Man's Guide for Personal Success
Emotional Wellness for Women Volume I
Emotional Wellness for Women Volume II
Emotional Wellness for Women Volume III
The Baby Boomer's Handbook for Women

Christian Series
The Power of God
The Power of God: Daily Devotional

These books are available from the individual contributors, the publisher (www.pwnbooks.com), www.amazon.com, and your local bookstore by request.